out in the
garden

Out in the Garden

Dean Riddle

...growing a beautiful life

Illustrations by Jeffrey Fulvimari

HarperCollins*Publishers*

For my parents, up there.
And for Barbara Epler, who said,
"Just write, the book will come out."

HarperCollins books may be purchased for educational, business, or sales promotional use. For information, please write: Special Markets Department, HarperCollins Publishers Inc., 10 East 53rd Street, New York, NY 10022.

FIRST EDITION

Designed by Jessica Shatan

Printed on acid-free paper

Library of Congress Cataloging-in-Publication Data

Riddle, Dean.
    Out in the garden : growing a beautiful life / by Dean Riddle ; illustrations by Jeffrey Fulvimari.—1st ed.
      p. cm
    ISBN 0-06-018805-7 (hardcover : alk. paper)
      1. Gardening—South Carolina—Mauldin. 2. Riddle, Dean. I. Title.
SB455 .R52 2002
635'.09757'27—dc21   2001039960

02 03 04 05 06 ❖/RRD 10 9 8 7 6 5 4 3 2 1

AUTHOR'S NOTE

I once worked in a New York restaurant with a charming Frenchwoman who was always curious about my life in the Catskills. One night she asked, "How is your house and garden? What do you do in your country life?" "Oh, this and that," I answered. "Sometimes I just gaze at the mountains or watch the catbirds playing." A regular customer (a man who owned three houses and around three hundred cashmere sweaters), sitting nearby, overheard our conversation: "So, Dean, I take it the lobotomy *was* a success."

table of contents

1. _Southern Exposure_ 1

2. _Nursery School_ 19

3. _Roots_ 53

4. _Sticks and Stones_ 59

5. _Learning the Ropes_ 87

6. _Branching Out_ 107

7. _Common Threads_ 131

8. _Basic Black_ 151

9. _Pots and Pans_ 163

10. _Work Detail_ 179

11. _Between Friends_ 195

12 _On the Porch_ 211

13. _The View_ 233

I hear some people have their dreams;
I've got mine.
I hear the mountains are doing fine,
The morning glory is on the vine.

—Neil Young "Motion Pictures"
(from the album *On the Beach*)

We're here for five minutes,
it has *got* to look good.

—Howard Christian

1 Southern exposure

MY PARENTS COULD REMEMBER when Mauldin, South Carolina, was just a wide place in the road. A crossroads set down in cornfields, with a Baptist church and a gas station, midway between Laurens and Greenville, a place on the way to somewhere else. It's hard to imagine it was ever like that; Mauldin has grown like nobody's business. Now it's a suburban mess of strip malls, fast-food restaurants, and giant video stores, where everybody seems to be parking or eating or waiting in traffic. I expect you'd have to drive a ways to find a cornfield.

The last vestige of small-town charm disappeared more than twenty years ago, when the Watleys died and their house, on the corner of Main and Butler, was demolished to make room for a BP station. Some shortsighted fool wiped that fine old brick house from the face of the earth like somebody swatting a fly. I hated to see that house destroyed, and the yard and gardens around it. There were towering southern magnolias with enormous, perfumed blossoms the color of old ivory; great dark camellia bushes with shiny, leathery leaves and voluptuous red flowers in the wintry months of the year; sturdy water oaks casting their cooling shade; and lacy spiraeas, sweet mock oranges, and other old-fashioned shrubs.

My parents didn't really garden, just kept the yard pretty. I suppose Mama was too busy raising children and keeping house to fool much with flowers. Besides, she never was an outdoor type and didn't cotton much to getting dirty. Daddy had a sizable vegetable patch when we lived in North Carolina, where I was born, but in Mauldin, apart from a couple of largely unsuccessful attempts at growing tomato plants, he never messed with vegetables again. I recall him complaining about the sticky red clay soil and fretting about an infestation of nematodes before he finally gave up on homegrown tomatoes.

It was in a spot at back of the house, near the carport and just by the kitchen door, where the plants had languished and died. Later on, Mama decided she wanted to try roses there, so Daddy bought a few bushes and stuck them in the ground. I remember thinking it was very tasteful and clever of my mother wanting to grow roses—it sounded so civilized and elegant. But that effort proved even less fruitful. I was so disappointed, as summer wore on, to see those flowerless canes sticking sadly out of the ground, with a piddling few dull green leaves hanging on for dear life. It wasn't long before the tomato-bed-turned-rose-garden was smoothed over and seeded with grass, to blend with the rest of our ordinary suburban yard.

After that, Daddy stuck to the basics. There was a row of assorted Japanese hollies growing along the front of our house, planted, I feel sure, by the building contractor as part of the suburban package. My father kept these predictable dwarf shrubs trimmed into lopsided balls, just like all the other lopsided green balls in front of all the other brick houses up and down the streets of our neighborhood. Our yard wasn't big, perhaps a quarter of an acre. And apart from a narrow strip of woods that ran along two sides, separating us from the neighbors, it was mostly just grassy lawn, punctuated with a few good native oak trees that the contractor had had the good sense to leave.

Daddy fussed with that lawn for years, trying to conquer the perennial wild onions that popped up by the millions every spring, driving him to distraction. On Saturdays, my twin brother and I were required to get down on our hands and knees and dig up the endless clusters of tiny white bulbs. Our father would appear every few minutes to admonish us against carelessness, knowing that every bulb left in the ground would flourish anew, creating a vigorous colony of the hated weed. Every chance I got I'd run inside for something to drink and whine to Mama about Daddy's obsession with those blasted onions.

But the absolute worst instance of forced labor perpetrated by my father occurred on a boiling hot Saturday in July of 1971. He had my brother and me grubbing out the most gigantic (or so it seemed at the time) tree stump you've ever seen. This was far from plain old everyday onion digging. My Lord in heaven! I felt like a prisoner on a chain gang. But what made it so bad, what made it, to my 13-year-old mind, so incomprehensible, was that we were engaging in this heinous work on the day after my Granny Hudson's death. Have mercy! There was my beloved grand-  mother laid out in Kennedy Mortuary in Laurens, Mama out shopping for a dark dress for the funeral, and us in the yard, slaving and sweating at a time like this. Why, I felt like the last heathen on earth. And I let my father know it, too, with my huffing and puffing and carrying on. I'm surprised he didn't jerk a knot in me, but I suppose he felt sorry for his boys having lost their grandmother. Of course, I was just being downright lazy—and righteous, to boot. It's funny, but with Daddy gone for over two years now, and Granny Hudson dead for thirty, I'd love to dig onions or grub out a stump for him today, in that yard on Elm Drive.

I suppose the closest thing to a real garden in our immediate neighborhood was next door at the Petersons. Of course, the Millers, a friendly couple who lived at the other end of our street, did keep a very respectable yard, planted with handsome dogwoods and crepe myrtles, and neat shrub beds mulched with pine straw, where they set out brightly colored pansies in the fall. And Mr. Miller took great pride in a small vegetable garden at the rear of their house. But we didn't know the Millers well, and they had no children my age to play with, so my experience of their garden was limited to my observations from the street. I remember admiring perfect, weed-free rows of turnip greens, collards, and corn as I cruised by on my bike.

Nick Peterson, who was slightly younger than I, was my best friend in those early years. We ran and played together constantly, so I was often in his yard. Like us, the Petersons had a number of big oak trees growing on their property. Beneath some of them, on large sprawling mounds of acid-rich soil, Nick's mother grew lush azaleas in hot, vivid shades of pink and red. And flowing around her house were fancy little brick-edged beds filled with a marvelous jumble of blue bearded iris and crimson sweet williams, with clean white candytuft spilling from the sides. I would've been around eight years old then, and I reckon it was the first time I really noticed a grouping of plants that had been consciously arranged together to create a pleasing picture. I can close my eyes this minute, plop down on the green grass in Nick's yard, reach out my hand in the warm spring sunshine, and touch those glorious blue iris. The long-ago smell of those spicy sweet williams and the curious beauty of their pinked petals is real, as real as the air I'm breathing today. I thought those flower beds were the prettiest things I'd ever seen. And I suppose they were. Because when something good and lasting happens in your soul—when the thing takes root and blossoms and holds its color—it simply doesn't get any better.

Central Avenue, the Petersons' street, marked the end of our neighborhood. Across from their place, behind a facing row of houses, lay mysterious woods and fields—an enchanted jungle full of oaks and hickories and green briar vines, where thin, meandering creeks swimming with crawdads and minnows gurgled softly and trickled over rocks, bound for some great river. Pretty little ferns grew along the mossy wet banks, and slivers of glassy mica sparkled magically in the water when the sun shot down from above.

Nick and I used to play out there like crazy, chasing through the woods and making up games. Sometimes we'd get up to no good, smoking cigarettes we had stolen from his mother. In warm weather we'd find a good spot in the sunshine, take off our clothes, and lie down on the ground. We knew this was being naughty. But of course, there was nothing in the world wrong with it. It was as natural to us as breathing, as natural and healthy as my fascination with the odd little pipsissewa plants, sprouting from the earth nearby, turgid and green and pulsing with life.

Back in those days the woods and fields seemed to stretch on forever, a fantastic wonderland of sensuous delights. Now they're gone forever, replaced by cramped neighborhoods full of dreary houses that my brother says nobody lives in for very long. Our house, sold now, following my parents' deaths in recent years, was nothing fancy. But it was solid and well built, with hardwood floors, good kitchen cabinets, and deep porcelain sinks in the bathrooms. And Daddy, like most of our neighbors, took care of our house, so it fetched a good price when it was sold.

Now the average house built for a middle-class family is flimsy and cheap. I always wonder who will live in them thirty years from now, when they're dingy and decrepit and falling apart. I know it'll be a cold day in hell when the powers that be have the wisdom to plan suburbia with any kind of foresight. Greenville, South Carolina, like dozens of other southern cities, has exploded in the past twenty years. Yes, the economy, that holy barometer of American culture, has prospered. But no matter how you slice it, the ruination of the once-bucolic landscape is disturbing.

Thank heavens, nearby Laurens County is still largely rural, much like it was when I was a child. We traveled there often to see my daddy's mother, Granny Riddle. It wasn't a long drive at all, perhaps thirty miles—"just a little piece down the road," is how Mother would have described it. But when I was real young it seemed like the longest trip in the history of the world. Like driving to I don't know where— maybe Egypt! I'd pester my mother to death: "When will we get there? Are we almost there? How much further is it, Mama." Lord knows, she must have had the patience of Job to put up with me. Of course, I knew every crook in the road like the back of my hand—knew by heart every country church and sagging shack along the kudzu-covered roadsides. Restless and fidgety, my brother and I would pick at each other in the back seat of the car until Daddy got fed up and pulled over. His right hand would come flying like some crazy mean bird from the front seat, to thump us on our heads and put a stop to our foolishness.

One time, years after Granny Riddle died but before I was old enough to really appreciate what I was seeing, my father drove along a road unfamiliar to us to show us where he had grown up during the Depression. There was nothing there but a piece of falling-down old barn, visible from the road, brown and weathered and swallowed up by wildness. For some reason, I wanted that barn to be what was left of his family's house. But Daddy said the house was long gone—torn down or burned down or otherwise destroyed. I've never seen his old home place again. But I'd like to think that barn is still standing, nestled in the same dense, leafy thicket of Chickasaw plum bushes that seemed that day to be guarding it for posterity.

I suppose that would have been the same barn he referred to one pleasant February day in the last winter of his life, when he and I were out walking together near his house. I had noticed a fine pair of persimmon trees growing in a neighbor's yard, still hung with a few shriveled old fruits from the previous autumn. When I commented that the native persimmon, with its beautiful, deeply fissured bark and graceful branching habit, was one of my favorite trees, he stopped his slow, deliberate shuffle, lifted his gaze to the persimmon trees, and said, "I guess they are right purdy, now that you mention it." "Did y'all eat wild persimmons when you were a boy?" I asked my father. "We ate a few, not many," was his reply. "But now, I'll tell you what—there was a big black walnut tree up by the barn on our place, and we ate right many o' them nuts. Gave some away, too. We grew potatoes in mulch piles, over by the barn. In the fall, we'd mound old cornstalks over 'em to protect 'em from the cold, you know. Then on a purdy day, when a breeze'd come up, we'd go out and bring a few inside and fix 'em to eat." That was all he had to say about that. He turned his stiff old frame around and started back to the house.

Granny Riddle lived with her only daughter and eldest child, Kathleen, and her husband, Roy. Uncle Roy was the quietest, gentlest man I have ever known. He was tall—tall as a tree to my child's eyes—and he had enormous hands. Mama used to say he was a fine, fine person, the salt of the earth, and everyone knew it was so. Aunt Kat, who never had any children, wasn't the easiest person in the world to get along with, but she was fiercely devoted to her mother, and to her brothers and their respective families. In the years before Granny Riddle died, and for a time afterward, their farm—a few miles away from where my father grew up—was the main gathering place for the Riddle clan.

And boy, they had some kind of vegetable garden. A good thing too—it took a pile of food to feed our crowd. My uncle grew everything in the book—okra, tomatoes, string beans, squash and cucumbers, peppers and corn, the best cantaloupe you ever put in your mouth, and great big watermelons. More than once I saw him take one of those juicy melons, icy cold from the fridge, and crack it open with his huge fist for us children to gorge on.

Mama would tell you right quick that Roy's tomatoes were the best she'd ever tasted. Like most people, she loved them simple, sliced on a plate with salt and pepper. In winter, when we had to make do with the hard, flavorless things from the grocery store, she'd shake her head in disgust. "I sure do wish I had one of Roy's good summer tomatoes," she'd say longingly, as she sprinkled on more salt. Mama always served her tomatoes on an oval glass plate, rose-colored with a decorative zigzag edge. The plate belongs to me now. When I place it on my table in summer, with bright red

tomatoes on an oval glass plate, rose-colored with a decorative zig zag edge.

tomatoes arranged on it, my heart is pleased down deep. Part of me is sitting down to Sunday dinner at home, while Mama, still dressed in her church clothes, hums a favorite hymn, pours the iced tea, and takes hot rolls from the oven.

My Aunt Kat was a hardworking person. In garden season she canned fruits and vegetables like crazy, in a small summer kitchen that was partially subterranean. I used to slip in there when nobody was around to escape the sticky summer heat, be by myself, and rest from playing. It was cool in there, like a cave. It felt safe, and there was a soothing silence about the place. It was dim, but not totally dark; a long, narrow window along the front wall, just below the ceiling, admitted some light for working. Like the rooms of her house, Kat's summer kitchen was tidy and well organized. There was a big double sink for washing vegetables in and assorted canning equipment on some of the shelves that lined the walls. The other shelves were filled with empty mayonnaise jars and store-bought Mason jars, too. Out of that room came frosty green bread-and-butter pickles, crisp and crunchy and so sweet they'd make your teeth hurt; rich red tomato juice; perfect, slender green beans for cooking with potatoes in winter; and sugary fig preserves that my daddy loved to slather on toast.

My aunt and uncle grew various flowers, shrubs, and potted plants. In his vegetable garden, on flat ground in full sun, where plants were arranged in long, straight rows, Roy left room for his tall bearded iris and bright, exuberant daylilies. How lovely the blossoming perennials looked in June and July, ranked along one edge of the garden beside the trellised beans and staked tomato vines. I used to wander slowly among those vibrant blooms, humming and daydreaming in a world of my own. In a separate area, on an expanse of lawn to one side of the driveway, my uncle had a small tea rose garden, invitingly furnished with a bench swing. In early spring, when the rose bushes emerged from dormancy, with tight bundles of coppery growth popping from their thorny canes, the earth around them sprouted with sweet-smelling jonquils.

Even as a child, I found it remarkable that this big, masculine man, with his calloused, hardworking hands, his knowledge of tractors and other machinery, his pickup truck and messy, oily tool room, took an interest in growing pretty flowers. I already had the sense that the world frowned on men who liked soft things, so it was touching and reassuring to see old Roy tending his perfumed irises and beautiful, fragrant roses. A friend of mine told me recently how her brother, a conservative fellow who lives in Texas, keeps his newfound love of gardening to himself, embarrassed by what his men friends might think if his secret were discovered. How very sad, I thought, that this man, who has opened his eyes to the sweet beauty of plants, is ashamed for others to know it.

Kat and Roy's house sat way back from the road they lived on and their large front yard was filled with garden shrubs of all kinds: nandinas and camellias; English boxwood, which Kat rooted from cuttings; evergreen hollies with red berries; pyracanthas and sasanquas; and azaleas everywhere. Ground-hugging patches of pink and lavender thrift flowered at Easter, when yellowbell bushes covered themselves with countless blossoms the color of egg yolks. Dotted around were Vanhoutte spiraeas, their arching branches smothered with dainty white flowers.

"Have you seen my white beautyberry?" Kat asked me one day, and off I went to have a look at this unusual shrub with its showy, porcelain-white berries gathered in tight clusters at every node along the branches. My aunt was particularly fond of her fringe tree, *Chionanthus virginicus,* a lovely native shrub in the olive family, decked in spring in a cloud of frothy-cream flowers whose delicate petals were as fine as silk thread.

On a shady porch at the front of the house Kat featured a collection of ferns, fancy-leafed begonias, and other potted foliage plants. These were arranged on a floor made of broken brick tiles that were set in concrete in a crazy-paving style. I used to love the coolness of that floor on my hot bare feet as I slid this way and that along the concrete seams, trying to establish some order in the confusing pattern of tiles. The porch was furnished with a metal glider and comfortable wooden rocking chairs for sitting out the oppressive summer heat. On Sunday afternoons, grown-ups relaxed there and passed the time, chatting and laughing about whatever came up. Mostly, the men sat slumped in their seats, dozing with their mouths dropped open, while the women discussed births and deaths, church goings-on, and the endless hot weather.

The woods around their place were rich with the deciduous broadleaf trees of the Southern piedmont. There was sweetgum, a cousin of witch hazel, with its corky, horizontal branches and decorative maple-like leaves that color so well in the fall, in muted tones of purple, orange, maroon, and gold. Stately tulip trees were abundant, their ramrod-straight stems reaching to the heavens. In early summer when the sculpted bowlshaped blossoms of this peculiar species would drift intact from the towering treetops, I'd collect them and float them in water, the better to marvel at the creamy flowers, their throats splashed green and orange. Oaks of every description grew there, and I loved every kind: water and willow oak; black and southern red; post oak and black jack; and the finest of them all, the majestic white oak, *Quercus alba*. There were sourwoods and tupelos; pin cherries and river birches; hickories, butternuts, and sycamores, too.

On one side of Kat and Roy's house, beneath a stand of tall, skinny pines that swayed and whispered in the wind, there was a picnic area with a view west, across an open meadow. Something happened there one day that will stay with me until I draw my last breath. I can't say how old I was, but I know I was just a little bitty thing, maybe four or five years old. And I know, too, that it was springtime, because I can vividly remember the gaudy pink hues of azaleas everywhere. There were lots of cousins and aunts and uncles there, and we were sprawled at tables and chairs under the pine trees, having a picnic.

I have no idea what I was doing—just playing, I suppose, engaged in the business of being a child. But for some reason, my grandmother, who was sitting nearby, called me a sissy or said I was acting like a girl. Well, she might just as well have slapped me across my face, bad as it hurt. I was utterly stunned. But I didn't cry. I simply climbed into the safety of my big sister's lap, where she hugged me close to her body. And having witnessed our grandmother's taunting, my sister—my protector—glared at her and scolded her; this was brave and outrageous behavior for a girl of per-

i know i was just a little bitty thing...

... but i can vividly remember the gaudy pink hues of azaleas everywhere.

haps fifteen. I can't possibly imagine why my grandmother chose to pick on me in such a way. It was totally uncharacteristic behavior for this person I trusted. For many years, whenever I allowed the memory of that day to surface, the conjured image of that old woman's broad, wrinkled face, the laughing and teasing in her voice, loomed large and monstrous in my mind.

But at forty-four years old I no longer find the image monstrous. It began to change and mellow and soften quite suddenly one day when, at age twenty-three, I sat down alone on a couch in Atlanta, Georgia, and said to myself out loud: "You are gay. You are fine. The world has been feeding you a bullshit line." It was both the hardest and the easiest thing I had ever done, and immensely relieving. Now when the childhood memory of that spring day returns, I welcome it with the open arms of experience and forgiveness. Today my grandmother's face, frozen in time in a haze of pink azaleas, is benign and sweet, indicative of the good, caring, and amusing person our family loved so dearly.

Perhaps I even owe my grandmother a debt of gratitude. For it was in the midst of that springtime picnic that I realized for the first time that someone else knew I was different from most other people in my small world. Until then I had thought it was my secret, if I bothered to think of it at all. Frankly, my sensitive ways had never stopped me before. And as I grew older, my parents never once asked me to be anyone I wasn't. When I asked for a baton for Christmas one year, it was lovingly given, and I went outside to proudly twirl it and prance about like some glamorous majorette. Still, as the years wore on, and long after I came out in my personal life, I never discussed my homosexuality with my parents. I took the easy way out simply because it was available to me in order to avoid confrontation and an unpleasant family situation. For this, I am ashamed.

On that sunny Carolina day, as I sat contentedly in Phyllis's lap and turned away from my grandmother's teasing, I was soothed and lulled and embraced by the natural, physical world. Like somebody floating on air, I drifted into the piney green treetops, looked down at the bright azaleas and out to the spring-fresh meadow. I didn't hurt anymore, I didn't cry a drop; I only breathed and knew who I was. I'd love to know what I did to provoke my grandmother's comment. But it doesn't matter, because I wasn't *acting* like a girl, I was simply *being* myself. And it was wrong for an intelligent woman in her sixties to ridicule a child who did nothing but worship her.

How peculiar that we live in a world so stunted and cold that an ordinarily generous and caring person—a grandmother of fifteen, no less—can find it somehow acceptable to crush the feelings of a little boy and rather fiendishly enjoy the outcome. Perhaps I knew in some tiny cell that Granny was the childish one that day. Perhaps my forgiveness of her began the very moment she rendered the blow. Because as I lingered on my sister's lap, filling my nostrils with the rich smell of pine trees and my soul with the breadth and blue of the sky stretched over the meadow, I still loved my Granny. I simply didn't understand her.

Several years later, when I was eleven years old, my grandmother died. I never quite understood just what her problem was, but she was miserably ill for months. "What's wrong with Granny," I asked my mother. "Honey, the doctor says she's got a growth inside of her the size of a grapefruit." And that's precisely what I pictured: a big, round, bad yellow grapefruit down in my grandmother's gut. Her funeral, at a country church near where she had reared her family, was the first I ever attended. We sang the old Baptist hymn "It Is Well with My Soul," a song we would sing again, many years later at both my parents' funerals:

When peace, like a river, attendeth my way,
When sorrows like sea billows roll;
Whatever my lot, thou hast taught me to say,
It is well, it is well with my soul.

The last memory I have of my grandmother when she was still healthy, is a vibrant and happy one. It's springtime again, a green Saturday morning, and we're slowly pulling up in our white Chevrolet to the back of Kat and Roy's house. And there is Granny, just beyond the fig bush in the backyard, picking strawberries in the garden. It's sunny and breezy and she is bent to her work, wearing a big straw hat and a billowy cotton dress. As I go bounding out of the car and into the garden, she stands and straightens and reaches out, and I dive into her arms. Later we go into the kitchen, where she cuts the strawberries into small pieces and drowns them with sugar. After placing three bowls of the glistening fruit on the table, she sits down with my brother and me and insists on hearing about all that's happening in our important lives.

2 nursery School

WHEN I WAS A SENIOR at Mauldin High School my best friend was Donna Ford, who lived a few streets away in our neighborhood. Donna got me started collecting houseplants. We were both big potheads and loved nothing more than to smoke a fat joint, jump in her VW, and zoom off to a greenhouse. Up and down the aisles we would go, agonizing over which plants to purchase with our paltry sums of money, giggling uncontrollably and having the most marvelous time as we feasted our eyes on lush tropical foliage.

Before long I had quite a collection going, and my mother was happy for me to display some of them around the house. So I featured jade plants, prayer plants, snake plants, and philodendrons here and there on tabletops, in empty corners, and in hanging baskets in sunny windows.

But most of my plants figured smartly in the elaborate décor of my bedroom, mingled in with old bottles, incense burners, and peace symbols. These items were set against a backdrop of black-light posters and a red, white, and blue color scheme. I thought it all looked *just* fabulous.

My plant obsession carried right into twelfth-grade art class, where I shared a table with Donna. I made a macramé plant hanger out of dark brown rope. It consisted of a wide panel of woven X's suspended from a bamboo rod. Near the bottom, where the X's ended, the remaining strands of thin rope came together in a configuration of knots that formed three holders for pots. I worked on that project with great diligence and concentration and when it was finished I thought it was magnificent. Mama did too. Or at least she pretended to. She let me hang that thing on the wall in the den as if it were something from Ivey's Department Store. "Oh, Dean, honey, I like that!" she exclaimed, without a trace of insincerity in her voice. How good it was of my mother to applaud my creativity so enthusiastically.

Donna and I remained inseparable for a while after high school and eventually enrolled at Greenville Tech to study accounting. Don't ask me how such a cockamamie idea came over us. In my case, it was like putting a fish on a bicycle. I was the first to bail after only a few weeks. Donna was no more interested in accounting than I, but she remained in school a while longer, because she had met Paul, a boy whose dreamy-eyed good looks and charming personality made me as nervous as all get out. They fell in love and got married, seemingly overnight, and I was left with nothing but my plant-collecting hobby.

What did I do? Moped around and felt sorry for myself. "Mama, what in the world am I going to do?" I whined to her one day, for the fiftieth time. She looked at me with concern, and said, "Dean, honey, I declare, you have got to get a hold of yourself and pull out of this slump. Why, my goodness gracious, you've got a good head on your shoulders and plenty to offer the world. You seem to love plants and being outside. Why don't you go get yourself a job in a nursery?" So that's what I did. I got in my two-tone Chevy Nova and drove up the Laurens Road to Greenville, went directly to Greer Nursery, one of the places Donna and I had shopped for houseplants, and got hired on the spot.

Greer Nursery was a typical retail garden center with an ordinary selection of plants—annuals, of course, and trees and shrubs such as magnolias, Japanese hollies, nandinas, camellias, junipers, and azaleas. Azaleas galore—the kind that come in cherry red and candy pink, and hot, glaring white and get shoved up against brick houses all over the South, as if there were no other plants to choose from in the world. The selection of perennials amounted to little more than a ragtag bunch of hostas and daylilies, lurking on the sidelines; this was in the days before perennials became hot items. There was a small shop with potting soil and fertilizer and a few houseplants and tools for sale. My job boiled down to three basic tasks: loading plants and other purchases into customers' cars, unloading delivery trucks, and watering—lots and lots of watering, which I enjoyed.

The business was owned by a man named Doug Taylor, who was rarely on the scene. He had another, larger nursery across town that occupied most of his time where he grew some of the plants we sold. Mr. Taylor was a big, middle-aged man with pale skin, thick glasses, and thin, flyaway hair. He was shaped like a giant pear and his clothes didn't fit properly, so he was forever hitching up his enormous, high-waisted trousers, which appeared to be belted right below his chest. When Mr. Taylor dropped by, I made myself scarce; he had a way of ignoring me that made me feel nervous and unimportant. But, at eighteen, I didn't much care what he thought. Eighteen-year-olds think they know everything and believe that adults beyond a certain age—say, twenty-five, tops—are absolutely out of the loop when it comes to anything of real importance, like music, clothes, and having fun.

The nursery was managed by a likable woman named Ballas Davis, whom I called Mrs. Davis. It would no more have occurred to me to call her Ballas than it would've come into my head to fly to the moon; it's the sort of thing that simply wasn't done when I was growing up. She called me "Young-un" from the day I set foot in the place and if she ever once spoke my real name, I don't recall it. Mrs. Davis was probably only in her fifties at the time, but she seemed old as the hills to me. She was a bird, tickled me to death, and in the several months I worked on the nursery I grew very fond of her.

Twenty-five years later, I can picture her crystal clear. She was of average height and slightly on the heavy side. She had high cheekbones, a sweet, fleshy face with wrinkles, and blue eyes that sparkled. Her hair was light brown flecked with gray, and every Friday she popped around the corner to Just Cuttin' Up to have it washed and set, maybe trimmed, returning with a bounce in her step and a smile on her face. She wore homemade polyester pants, sensible lace-up shoes, and smocks with pockets, in which she kept her cigarettes and lighter—that woman sucked down Belair cigarettes like they were going out of style.

I was the only full-time employee other than Mrs. Davis. But on Saturdays we were joined by two college-aged brothers—fraternal twins, who were both as tall as trees and as blond as beach sand. One of them was sweet-natured and friendly and cute as pie—I got along fine with him. But the other boy was a real smarty-pants, with a dumb-jock attitude, who tried to make me feel second rate. It usually worked because he was bigger and older.

Those boys lived and breathed basketball like there was no tomorrow. I couldn't have cared less about sports of any kind. I felt like a displaced person on Saturdays. And I was none too happy about the special affection Mrs. Davis appeared to have for the boys. They got to do unusual, fun things, like wash her fancy Chevrolet Caprice. She even let them drive it on occasion. When I asked to drive it one time, she looked at me like I was insane. "Oh, *no*, Young 'un, that's a *nice* car," she said, like it was a solid gold Rolls Royce.

One morning we received a shipment of Japanese hollies, and the twins and I were put to work unloading them. The plants were small but respectable, in gallon pots, and there were more than a hundred of them. Back and forth we went, from the truck to the nursery beds, arranging the plants in rows. But the longer we worked, the more I noticed the hollies were a bit feathery and sparse. I decided they needed some pruning to make them branch out. The boys offered not a word of protest when I presented my plan. So, without hesitation and pleased as punch with my quick thinking, I got on with what I felt to be very important work.

For a while I was utterly sure of what I was about. But gradually I began to get a sick, queasy feeling—the pruned hollies were not looking so good after all. They looked butchered—in fact, they *were* butchered! Oh, my Lord in heaven, I thought to myself, what on earth came over you? Desperately, knowing I was in too deep to turn back, I made the decision to continue. I reasoned that if I could quickly finish the job, Mrs. Davis would never know what the plants had looked like to begin with. But before I even had time to work up a good sweat and get really scared, Mrs. Davis appeared out of nowhere. I knew I was dead meat. She took one look at those poor hollies and went ballistic. I thought she was going to gouge my eyes out: "Young 'un!" she shrieked. "What in the name of Sam Hill do you think you're doing? Have mercy! I've got a good mind to blister your bottom. Now you get out back and water them pots and don't you miss a one!"

You can be sure I hightailed it out of there as fast as my feet would carry me. I was smarting something fierce and had wounds to lick. I lost myself in the rear forty, a sort of no-man's-land where discount plants—misfits and pot-bound trees and shrubs—were relegated to spend their last days or, if they were lucky, be discovered and rescued by curious customers who might venture into this bargain basement. I kept a decidedly low profile the rest of the morning and stuck to my watering, wondering how long it would take Mrs. Davis to forgive me.

When lunchtime rolled around I dropped my watering hose, tucked my tail, and headed out of the bushes to face the inevitable embarrassment. Well, you can imagine my delight—relief is more like it—when I found the twins had been given the afternoon off. Good. I wouldn't have to feel foolish and humiliated in their presence. Mrs. Davis tried to give me the cold shoulder at first, but she soon backed off. "Run get us some lunch, Young 'un," she said, handing me some cash, "and don't you drag them feet and take all day." Her buying lunch was a good sign. I knew things were looking up.

I trotted off to Pete's Drive-In a few blocks down the street, returning directly with two Steakfinger Plates, our favorite thing on the menu. We ate together in silence, enjoying our greasy, ketchup-slathered food and bottles of cold Mountain Dew. Afterward, she sat smoking a Belair, gazing out the window at the parking lot while I talked a blue streak about everything under the sun. Then suddenly, as though emerging from a fog, she stubbed out her cigarette, and roared "Young 'un, get outside and make yourself useful 'fore I have to fire you and rehire you. Mr. Taylor'd skin us both alive if he came walkin' in here right now!" As I went bounding into the sunshine to resume my watering, I knew I had been forgiven.

Watering was my favorite chore and I spent hours and hours doing it. It was tricky at times to hit every single pot, particularly when working in the rear of the nursery, where everything was jumbled and messy, but I always made sure each plant got a good, good drink. Whenever possible, I like doing things thoroughly, right down to the last detail. I'm

"...but I always made sure each plant
got a good, good drink."

this way when I make up my bed, put apples in a bowl, or balance my checkbook. A friend of mine used to tease me when he'd catch me moving a couple of candlesticks and a vase of flowers around on a table for five minutes. But what can I say? I have to wait for my eye to give me the thumbs up. "Fine, good, well done, my dear and faithful slave. That's perfect. Now move on to the next discordant thing and make it sing for you." Details add up.

I still love hand watering and always will. There is something so good and essential about this simple thing gardeners do for the plants they cherish. When I'm forced to be away from my garden in summer, my friend and neighbor Amy is kind enough to water for me in my absence, thus earning a very high place in my heart. While I'm away, I imagine her among my plants and hope she is happy in her work. But I know she is, because when I return, she will tell me how much she enjoyed doing this thing, and she will tell me again and again and again, all the while saying the loveliest things possible about my garden. It delights me to know that she takes such pleasure in my garden, and I find it hard to adequately express my appreciation. So I become quiet, but inside, I am ever, ever so grateful. I hope Amy knows this and never feels for a moment that I take her generosity for granted. Having a good neighbor is a wonderful, comforting thing.

I think it was during my hours of watering at Greer Nursery that I began to truly fall in love with plants and the natural world. Out in the hot sun among the growing things, I had only my thoughts and dreams to keep me company, and I marveled at the various shapes and colors of the leaves and blossoms, the ways and habits of the stems and branches, the buds and roots, the smells, the life and death of it all. This was when I began to want to know more and more and more. Why were these plants here? Where did they come from in the world? And most of all, what were their names—their *real* names?

Mrs. Davis called everything by its common name. I knew plants had scientific names, but I didn't realize that it was unprofessional of her not to know and use them. Her name for cotoneaster—a popular shrub in the rose family—was "Cotton Easter," and she wrote it exactly in that way, double quotes and all, on the wooden labels she put in the pots. I can see the labels now and the crooked letters in black ink. I liked this funny, sweet name, and I did not like it, too. I liked it because it made me think of white bunnies, ladies in pretty new hats, and poor Jesus on the cross before he floated up to heaven. But I didn't like it because it told me nothing about the plant. I knew this name could not possibly be taken seriously by too many people other than Mrs. Davis. I can just hear her now, talking to a customer, "Yes, ma'am, 'at's called Cotton Easter—'bout as easy to grow as fallin' off a log. It'll bloom-out right purdy for you in springtime and get berries in fall. Give it plenty o' sun."

I remember little about my last days at Greer Nursery. But one moment stands out clearly that involved a generosity of spirit on the part of Mrs. Davis that I shall never forget. The whole time I worked there I pestered her to give me a small glass pitcher I had found one rainy day while prowling through a back room of the shop. There was nothing fine or fancy about it in the least—I simply liked it. It was squat

simple
use of a
Cache pot

and clear, heavy for its size, with thin, vertical ridges, a shapely handle, and a narrow, tapered spout. Its very plainness was what appealed to me.

But my persistent begging got me nowhere. Mrs. Davis told me over and over how the pitcher wasn't hers to give away, that it belonged to Mr. Taylor and to *please, please* leave her alone and why in the *world* did I want it anyway? "Just because," I'd whine, "because I like it and I collect old bottles and other things and I just *know* it'll look real good with them. And Mrs. Davis, honestly, you know as well as I do Mr. Taylor doesn't even know that pitcher exists and wouldn't care a straw for it if he did." This was undoubtedly true. The room where I had discovered the pitcher was filled with junk that had been collecting dust for more years than I'd been walking on earth. Finally, on my last day, she presented me with the pitcher. "Here, Young 'un, I know how bad you want this thing. I'm gonna miss you, you stinker."

I treasured my gift for over twenty years. One Sunday morning not so long ago, I was making wild blackberry pancakes for some houseguests and was going to use the pitcher for warm maple syrup. When I removed it from its special place on a shelf in my kitchen, it slipped from my hand and shattered on my porcelain sink. I hated breaking something that meant so much to me, but while I cleaned up the broken glass, I thought of Mrs. Davis and smiled inside. I knew I would always have my cherished memory of her sweet gesture.

It was during my months at Greer Nursery that I decided to study horticulture. Someone had told me about Haywood Technical College, a small school in the mountains of western North Carolina that apparently had a very good horticulture department. So one day in the summer of 1977 I drove up and looked around the campus. I liked what I saw, made a few inquiries in the office, and left with a good feeling. A couple of weeks later I returned and took an entrance exam—and that was that. I never considered another school. I do a lot of things this way, partly because I can't stand to shop around, but mostly because I know better than to ignore my intuition. It's not a flawless method for living, but it works for me at least 90 percent of the time. A week before school was to begin in September, I found a tiny two-room apartment (three if you counted the bathroom) for $80 a month, in a mint green cinderblock building that had once been a motel. It was beside a four-lane highway, directly across from the college.

Early one Saturday morning, I loaded up my Chevy Nova with every stick I owned (not much), including a huge philodendron draped over boxes and bags piled high in the back seat, and left Mauldin, for North Carolina. Two hours later I pulled up to my new apartment. By midafternoon I had that place pulled together like nobody's business—clean as a pin, boxes unpacked, books on the shelves, pictures on the walls, and my bottle collection prominently displayed in the kitchen. And sunning in the front window was a lush Cleopatra begonia given to me by my Aunt Kat. I was out on the small front porch by sundown—Mr. Fancy Pants—loving my brilliant mountain view, listening to *Sticky Fingers* and sipping on Chivas Regal. (Back then I thought sophistication was all about scotch on the rocks. Now I get sick to my stomach if I come near the stuff.)

Haywood Tech was in a small, dull town called Clyde, in Haywood County, "Gateway to the Great Smoky Mountains." Apart from its horticulture course and a few other programs including textile design, fine woodworking, and jewelry making, all of which were led by good teachers, it was a rather undistinguished school. One of the more unusual courses was for professional sawyers—people in the lumber business—and it attracted students from all over the country. Several boys in this group lived in my building.

Take Jerry, for example, whose daddy owned a lumber mill in the boondocks of Mississippi. Now there was a crazy hellion if ever there was one. Jerry cruised around in a loud, jacked-up Grand Prix, looking for squirrels to squash. He chain-smoked cigarettes and guzzled Budweiser beer. A tall stack of porn magazines lay on the floor of his living room beside a plaid lounge chair placed smack in front of a TV that ran nonstop. His place was an ungodly mess—that boy was so utterly clueless about housekeeping it was sad. Poor Jerry appeared dumbstruck every time he stepped into my tidy apartment.

Once in a while, when I was desperate for money, I'd clean house for him, a gruesome task I'd rather not recall in detail. He always seemed to have plenty of cash, and I figured his parents sent him all that extra spending money just to keep him four states away. Still, Jerry was a good person at heart—apart from the squirrel killing, which, to his extreme amusement, sent me into a screaming fit when I rode with him—and he was generous with me. I used to insist on being taken out for a nice dinner after scrubbing that nasty apartment of his, and he willingly complied.

A few doors down lived Thomas, a tall, skinny boy from Pennsylvania who could hardly have been more different from Jerry. He was quiet and reflective, he read books, and his place was clean and homey. Once a week or so, he'd invite me over for dinner and serve delicious green salads, crunchy with almonds and bean sprouts, or savory hot soup with homemade bread and red wine. He always set the table attractively and even used cloth napkins. He placed candles round the room and played record albums softly while we ate together. Rita Coolidge was one of Thomas's favorite singers.

And then there was Cliff—dear, adorable Cliff with beautiful, deep brown eyes and an incurable sweet tooth. He lived at the rear of our building, and it seemed that every time I turned around, he was coming through my back door with a plate of warm chocolate chip cookies. "Hey, Dean-o, I thought you might like some cookies," he'd announce brightly. I'd put the kettle on the stove and sit down at the kitchen table with him. Cliff had come all the way from Vermont to attend Haywood Tech, and he talked endlessly about how he couldn't wait to get back home to his fiancée, Abbie.

He graduated before I did, and during a summer break, not long after he returned to New England, I got on a Greyhound bus and went to visit him. This was my first trip north of the Mason-Dixon line. During an afternoon stopover in New York, where it was hot as pigs, I wandered out of the Port Authority bus terminal and onto the sidewalk for a glimpse of the big city. Not five minutes into my adventure a large, round prostitute, barely clothed in a tight pink getup, leaned from a doorway, and said, "Hey, there, sweet boy, do ya need anythang?" Oh, Lord! I turned my country butt around fast and bolted back to the bus station. When I got to Cliff's house in Vermont later that night, he had stepped out briefly, and there was a note on the screen door: "Welcome, Dean, come in and make yourself to home."

I wonder if Cliff ever had any inkling of the terrible crush I had on him. Not that it matters—he clearly had eyes only for Abbie. I'm not sure even I knew the truth of it; I didn't allow myself to believe that the affection I felt for this handsome boy was erotic love. At twenty years old, I was so firmly, stupidly ensconced in my dark closet that if Cliff had stripped naked and pounded on its door, I probably would have pretended not to hear.

I'll never forget when my friend Deborah, a fellow horticulture student at Haywood Tech, asked with open curiosity one day, quite out of the blue, if I had ever thought of having a boyfriend. (Bless her heart—she obviously had my number.) "Oh, no, never," I said firmly, and with feigned horror. Three years later, sitting in her kitchen on a winter day, I came out to her; she could not have been more loving and understanding. Patrick, her husband, was in the next room at the time and Deborah simply called out to him: "Patrick, honey, Dean's gay." His response: "I know." I was a tad embarrassed by his easy frankness, but also touched and very amused. It felt good to know that these dear friends loved and accepted me totally for who I was. And with his casual "I know," Patrick seemed to be saying, in a sense, that my sexuality was about as important to him as the color of my eyes.

Deborah and I were constant companions at Haywood Tech. Our classes were structured around practical hands-on work in campus gardens, in the school greenhouses, and in various lab sessions. We studied everything from soil science to floriculture to plant pathology. My favorite courses were those in botany and plant identification. It was wonderful to finally be learning and understanding botanical nomenclature. We were helped in this by a student who was always trying to impress us with his brain full of trivia about plant and animal life. Once he pulled something out of his hat that was very clever. We were required to memorize the taxonomic classification hierarchy: Kingdom—Division—Class—Order—Family—Genus—Species—Variety—Form—Individual. He swaggered into class one day with the following acronym: Katy—Did—Come—Over—Friday—to—Get—Some—Vitamins—For—Ida. It was a perfect tool for remembering the exact order of the plant phyla. But I recently heard an amusing version for kingdom through species that I like even better: Kindly—Do—Come—Over—For—Gay—Sex.

Inspired by a brilliant teacher, David Carson, who was a walking encyclopedia of knowledge, Deborah and I fell hard in love with native plants, particularly the exquisite woodland wildflowers that grew in abundance in the lush mountains all around us. Mr. Carson was the first person to really open my eyes to indigenous plants. The first winter of school, nestled in my cozy apartment, I read constantly about the natural history of the southern Appalachians and combed through various field guides to trees, shrubs, and wildflowers. I bombarded Mr. Carson with questions that would spring to mind during my reading; never once did he appear to be anything other than totally available and willing to satisfy my curiosity.

That winter I realized I was living smack in the middle of one of the most diverse plant communities in the temperate world. As I browsed through books, my eyes would bore into photographs of pretty, delicate wildflowers, and I would think to myself, Can this be? Can all these botanical treasures actually be right here at my fingertips, slumbering in the cold earth, waiting to be seen and adored and fill me with awe at their delightful forms and beautiful colors?

When spring arrived and the mountains came to life I went absolutely crazy. I had never felt so completely alive. Had you offered me a ticket to anywhere, to the most exotic rain forest on the globe, I might have refused. I was in the most sublime place imaginable. Until then I had never seen the lovely, painterly gradations of color—pink, copper, and bronze—in the soft, green foliage that dresses the ancient mountains every spring. From that moment on the intense beauty of the southern Appalachians never left my eyes.

I live now in the Catskill Mountains in upstate New York, and it's a wonderful, marvelous place, but first love is first love and that's the plain truth. I've always thought that home ought to be the prettiest place in the world to a pair of eyes. How else can a person ever properly see another place in the world if he doesn't first know, with all his senses, the place he came from? The Carolina mountains where I was born will forever own my heart, whether I ever reside there again or not.

I spent hours exploring the woods in spring in search of the wildflowers I had seen in books. The first one I came upon was a lovely showy orchis (*Orchis spectabilis*). I dropped to my knees and fully onto my belly and chest and pushed my eyes in close, to marvel at the subtle beauty of this plant and the amazing construction of its parts. As I lay on the ground admiring the glossy basal leaves springing from the earth and the short flower stalk crowned with tiny, pink-hooded orchids with white lips, I touched my nose lightly to the blossoms and drew in deeply the sweet perfume. And it seemed for a moment that the sum total beauty of the planet Earth was held there in one precious, living thing. After that, I became rather obsessed with native orchids.

Deborah was just as crazy about wildflowers as I was. We regularly compared notes and fantasized about rare plants that we desperately hoped to encounter on our hikes through the woods. Topping our list was the incomparable showy lady's slipper orchid (*Cypripedium reginae*). We had a goofy routine that we performed over and over, when discussing this and other elusive flowers: "Now, Dean, be honest, be absolutely honest," Deborah would begin, earnestly. "Would you faint, would you just totally faint if you saw a showy lady's slipper orchid?" After a well-rehearsed pause, with eyes gazing thoughtfully into the distance, I would boom: "No! No! I would *not* faint, Deborah! I would *perish!*" And on cue, we would erupt into silly giggling and collapse together in a heap. Like us, Patrick was a lover of flowers, but he regarded us suspiciously, dubbing our strange affliction "wildflower frenzy." I'm sorry to report that I've still never seen the loveliest lady's slipper of them all.

Near the end of my two years at Haywood Tech, a Mr. Humphreys, the production director of a large and famous English nursery, came to our school for a few days to conduct a propagation workshop. I can't recall one single thing

I learned; perhaps I spent the time goofing off with Deborah. But one day he did manage to catch my ear—big time—when he told us about a one-year studentship program offered by his firm, Hillier Nurseries. During the coffee break that morning everyone was buzzing about going to England; in my mind I was already packing my bags. I told Deborah, "I'm going to work in that nursery as surely as I'm standing here today." Until then I had given zero thought to what I would do upon graduation. Suddenly the future had presented itself.

Mr. Carson gave a dinner party for Mr. Humphreys later in the week. Guess who got to go? My teacher was a marvelous cook who loved to entertain, and I was often invited to affairs in his home. Arriving early and leaving late, I would assist throughout the evening: taking coats, mixing drinks, serving food, and washing up dishes after. But Mr. Carson never treated me like a servant and I was always included in conversation. Cocktails and dinner parties, as such were new things to me (I grew up with iced tea and supper), and I took to that social, chatty business like a fish to water.

After dinner I pounced on Mr. Humphreys and bent his ear to death, drilling him with questions about the nursery studentship and describing in detail my qualifications as a candidate. He must not have minded too much, because by the end of the party I had squeezed a fairly firm commitment from him. After he returned home, and true to his word, he put the necessary papers in order. And before I had time to turn around and say boo, I had my work permit in hand. It was official. I was going to England.

When I called my parents with the news, Mama somehow got confused and thought I was talking about New England. When she finally got the story right and realized I would be going abroad for a year, she got a little stirred up and said, "Now, just hold your horses there a minute. I'm not so sure about all this." But she came round soon enough and was happy for me. As soon as classes ended at Haywood Tech, I packed up my belongings, left my apartment, and returned to South Carolina. My family gathered one Saturday to say good-bye and presented me with a set of luggage. A few days later, I put on a new V-neck sweater that I thought was out of this world, and my parents drove me to Atlanta and put me on a plane to London. Mama cried and I didn't. Not until I got on the plane.

After two days in London, during which time I mostly wandered around in confusion, I boarded what I called a bus and they called a coach and rolled off to Hampshire, where Hillier Nurseries were located, near the old city of Winchester. Along the way the driver stopped at every village we came to, but I could never quite understand him when he'd announce our arrival. So finally I got up my nerve, and from my seat I said, "Excuse me, please, sir, but have we gotten to Winchester yet?" About ten heads in front of me swiveled around in unison and twenty eyes looked at me like I had just beamed down from Mars. I must have sounded like Jethro Bodine or somebody else fresh out of the sticks. But the driver kindly assured me I had not missed my stop. I slumped back into my seat and tried to be inconspicuous.

When I got to Winchester nobody was there to meet me. Who did I expect, the Queen? But a nice young couple with two small children, seeing my predicament, offered to drive me to the nursery's youth hostel, where I was to live. It happened to be right on their way home. The people were as nice as could be, and we talked easily as the man drove along in the tiniest station wagon I had ever seen. After a while, the boy, who was perhaps five years old, asked me if I had ever been to Disneyland. I said, "No, I'm afraid not, but I have been to Six Flags Over Georgia." He was totally unimpressed and went right back to staring at me unabashedly. Shortly, I was delivered to the front door of Brentry House, the hostel, where the kind family wished me well and drove away in their toy car.

It was a lovely afternoon—Easter Sunday, in fact—but the hostel was silent when I stepped through the door. Presently, a short, old man with thick, white hair and horn-rim glasses appeared and introduced himself as Cyril, the hostel keeper. He explained that the other guys were working, even though it was Sunday, because the nursery was in the midst of the busy spring planting season and students were required to work overtime. After giving me a brief tour of the house and showing me to my room, which I would be sharing with another guy, he vanished. I was instantly homesick. There was nothing to do, however, but rise to the occasion. So I dropped my bags and raced outside.

The Hillier Arboretum, a vast collection of plants from all over the temperate world, was situated directly across the road from the hostel. I plunged in and wandered about for a couple of hours. There were hundreds of species there I had never seen; some of them I had read about. Of particular interest to me were the various Asian maples and magnolias, and oaks from many regions. It was comforting to see lots of familiar plants I knew from back home—amelanchier, fothergilla, liquidambar, sassafras, kalmia, and other American plants. The Hillier name is world-famous. For several generations the family business has distinguished itself by offering a mind-boggling range of plants. The arboretum functions as an outdoor classroom and also provides propagation material for the nursery. Frankly, the place was rather a mess when I was a student there. Little thought had been given to garden design, and trees and shrubs were planted arbitrarily wherever space allowed. But this was twenty years ago, so perhaps improvements have been made.

When I got back to Brentry House I had butterflies in my stomach. I knew the guys would be home from work and I was nervous about being the new kid on the block. As I opened the door I could hear a jumble of loud voices coming from the kitchen. Get it over with, I thought, as I moved in that direction. My stars above! You've never seen such an unruly bunch in all your life as that crowd of guys, clamoring for their dinner like a pack of hungry wolves. I stood awkwardly to one side, waiting to be noticed, wishing I could evaporate, while they hurried by with plates of food, on their way to the TV room. As the kitchen emptied out, the remaining few guys tossed me a nod or two and mumbled lukewarm introductions. But not one of them bothered to show me where the food was, on covered plates stacked in the oven. Thinking there wasn't a portion for me, I wandered into the TV room and took a seat. I was starving.

The person next to me instantly began a conversation, and

for that reason he holds a special place in my heart to this day. He wanted to know my name, where I was from, how my trip was, and what I thought of London. And all the while he kept on asking about my tea—"Have you had your tea? Don't you want your tea? Wouldn't you like your tea? Why don't you have your tea?"—until I thought I would knock him out of his chair. "No, I don't care for any tea," I said, over and over, "I really don't care for any tea, thank you, I really don't, no." About this time, I noticed the other guys grinning and whispering among themselves. We all had a good laugh when it was revealed to me that "tea" was the evening meal. I flew to the kitchen to find a solitary plate in the oven, heaped with leathery meat, dull potatoes, and a pile of dried-up something that vaguely resembled cabbage. Cyril hadn't forgot me after all. My homesickness was going away.

Monday morning, my first day on the job, was raw and wet. I was placed with a small group of students supervised by a tall, handsome man called Andy, a friendly fellow who made me feel comfortable right away. After receiving the standard issue provided by the nursery—Wellington boots, green rain gear, and Felco secateurs—I squeezed into a rickety van with several students and settled onto the grimy floor. As the van bumped along on its way to one of the planting fields, we rode in silence for a few minutes, until a young woman asked me politely where I was from in the States. "I'm from South Carolina," I answered, and every syllable that left my mouth sounded a mile long. "Oh, that's nice," she responded, "I was in Florida once." And she wanted to know if I knew her relative there. Everyone chuckled at this amusingly absurd question—except for one skinny boy, who sat stern-faced and brooding, stealing furtive glances at me from the corner.

I had been acutely aware of him since the day before, when I first saw him in the hostel. The moment our eyes met, his bore into mine like two headlights on a train from hell. Jeepers! What had I done? For several days, whenever we were together, you would have thought somebody was going to draw a knife. As it turns out, I was guilty of nothing more than being an American: Mick Richardson had a bad attitude about Yanks! Fortunately, he somehow came around, though I don't recall what happened. All of a sudden one day, the ice broke, and we became the best of friends. We had loads in common—we liked the same plants, music, books, movies, and social activities. He dubbed me "Grandiflora," as in *Magnolia grandiflora,* the lush evergreen tree emblematic of the American South. I'd be upstairs in my room in the hostel when I'd hear his voice trilling down the hallway: "Grrrr-andi-florr-a, where are you?" he'd call out, rolling his r's theatrically as if he were some grand matron. I'd drop what I was doing, and off we'd go to a pub or across the road to explore the arboretum together.

Mick completed his studentship before I did and returned to a horticultural college where he was enrolled. We stayed in touch regularly and I went several times to visit him at school. After I returned to the United States, we exchanged letters frequently for a couple of years, but our correspondence eventually lagged. One Christmas, realizing I hadn't heard from him in many months, I wrote him a long letter. Quite soon I received a response that shocked and saddened me. It came from his father in Yorkshire:

Mick had been dead for a year. After college, he had returned to Hillier's to work as a supervisor. One day, while he was dismantling a sprinkler system, he touched a high-voltage cable and was killed instantly. Mick's father wrote of the family's grief over the loss of their only son. I reread the letter repeatedly and have kept it to this day, along with the ones I received from Mick.

I wonder if the trees I once gave my friend still grow in England. During our time together at Hillier's, I would boast to Mick about the botanical riches of the southern Appalachians, and he would tease me ruthlessly about my obsession. So for Christmas that year I gave him a pair of American silverbells—*Halesia carolina* and *H. monticola*—and he planted the two saplings in his parents' garden. These elegant plants, whose bare branches are hung with snow-white blooms shaped like bells in spring, are superb trees for small gardens, where they lend themselves beautifully to underplanting with bulbs and perennials. As I sit today remembering Mick, I hope his trees have thrived and blossomed in the twenty years since they were first planted in a Yorkshire garden I have never seen.

Mick and I worked together almost daily in my first weeks at Hillier's. Planting season went on forever and the work was backbreaking and monotonous. Our crew of five worked together in one of the nursery's many fields for hours, planting rooted cuttings of various shrubs. The supervisor drove a tractor that pulled a planting mechanism mounted with three seats. There three students sat leaning forward, each facing a planting wheel that slowly turned as the tractor crept down the rows. Each planting wheel was fitted with evenly spaced collars that moved in sync with it. As an open collar came around, the student planter would place a cutting inside and the collar would snap shut, holding the cutting in place. As the wheel brought the collar into contact with the ground, the collar would pop open and release the tiny plant into the soil. And the wheel would turn another notch—over and over and over.

A fourth student walked along behind, straightening the plants in their rows and kicking soil to the roots, while firming the ground with his feet. He also toted a canvas bag that contained bundles of cuttings, which he handed to the planters as needed. This was an easier, more interesting job than planting and far less stressful on the back. (Fortunately, this job was rotated among the students.) It also carried with it just enough power to bring out the sadistic streak in anyone so inclined. Mick throve in this position: "All right, you sorry, useless little buggers, the cushy business is over. It's time for some real work!" And, cracking his imaginary whip, he would direct the driver to speed up, which would cause the planting wheels to turn faster and us planters to work even harder. We'd play along for a bit, begging for mercy and dreaming of reaching the end of the row, where we could dismount and stretch our weary bodies. But if our pleading went unheeded and the driver didn't slow down, one of us would simply say to the other two: "It's time." Then we would all three begin placing the cuttings upside down in the collars. As rows of roots sticking up in the air began to appear at his feet, Mick would suddenly start laughing and yelping. And the entire operation would be halted as the supervisor stopped the tractor and climbed down screaming, swearing he would have "the lot of you sacked."

At noontime we'd find a decent spot at the edge of the field, perhaps in the shade of a tree, plop down on the ground and open our box lunches from the hostel. Everyone would complain about Cyril's boring sandwiches and stale pastries, but we never left a crumb. We'd drain our thermos bottles of coffee or tea, and those who smoked would light up. Mick and I took our plantsmanship very seriously and always carried with us our dog-eared copies of *Hillier's Manual of Trees and Shrubs.* So after we finished eating, we'd browse the pages of our books while discussing our favorite species and cultivars and debating their merits. At the time—and perhaps still—*Hillier's Manual* was the bible for students and connoisseurs of woody plants. My old field copy is long gone, but a treasured hardback edition is in my library today, and I find it more useful than ever. Long after I left Hillier's, I read Russell Page's indispensable classic, *The Education of a Gardener,* and was delighted to learn that the great designer always kept a copy of *Hillier's Manual* close by.

When I was at the nursery, its third generation owner, Sir Harold Hillier, was in his eighties. He was no longer active in the daily operation of the business, but several times I saw him walking in the arboretum. I would follow at a respectful distance and watch him as he stopped at one plant after another, examining them intensely and jotting notes on a small pad of paper. I've wished a thousand times since that I had approached him and introduced myself, or requested a formal meeting in his home, as some students did. In his

day, Sir Harold was regarded as one of the greatest plantsmen that ever lived.

A couple of years after I returned to the United States, I heard about some people in northern Georgia, in a place called Little Bird Mountain, who had a major collection of native plants. I arranged for a visit and drove to see the couple on a spring day. They were cordial enough as they began to show me around their garden, but when I mentioned that I had been a student at Hillier's, you would have thought that I was some long-lost cousin risen from the dead. Before I knew what had hit me, I was seated at their kitchen table with a glass of sweet tea and a plump sandwich for lunch. It turns out they were old friends of Sir Harold and had even been to Mexico with him once on a plant-hunting expedition. The woman went so far as to show me the room in her house where Hillier had slept.

After the long planting season at the nursery ended, I was assigned various jobs during the summer, including labeling the very plants we had recently planted. In this job, which lasted several weeks, I worked with only one other person. Up and down the rows of the fields we'd go, tagging each block of plants with a bright yellow plastic label inscribed by us in black ink with the plant's name. This was pleasant, easy work that offered me the chance to observe in detail the characteristics of the various species and learn the exact spellings of their long Latin names. I was rather lucky to be entrusted with this important task.

But I suppose my favorite job of all at Hillier's came later, during the fall and winter "lifting season," when the fields crawled with students digging plants for shipping to customers in Britain and around the world. Occasionally, I worked on a wholesale crew, digging large orders of bare-root trees of only one or two species: for several days we might dig nothing but ashes, birches, or hawthorns. Fortunately, I spent most of the lifting season in the nursery's retail division, where the fields contained a much larger variety of plants. And I worked alone most days, which suited me fine.

In the mornings my supervisor gave me a stack of plastic labels of different colors. Each one was computer-printed with the necessary information—plant name, quantity, size, customer name, and address—pertaining to the plant or plants I was to dig for that particular order. The color of the label signified the eventual method of shipping—air, rail, post, or lorry. With labels in hand, I'd pick up my spade and satchel and head out to the fields for a day of digging.

The trees I lifted were all deciduous. Most were no more than 5 feet tall, and the majority of them were dug bare-root. The soil was quite loose and crumbly in the fields, and the plants came from the ground with minimal effort. But the nursery rows were tightly planted, so it was important to work carefully when digging a selected tree so as not to disturb the roots of neighboring plants. After thoroughly loosening the soil around a chosen tree, I'd grasp the base of the stem and, using my spade for leverage, gently tease the plant from the soil. It was pleasing to see the sinuous, fibrous root mass leave the ground, the rich smell of earth lingering in its wake. And it was very pleasurable indeed when the tiny white feeder roots appeared to be undisturbed—evidence of a job well done. A few plants, such as small oaks, hickories, and walnuts, had to be lifted with root balls. This was more tedious and time-consuming work, but I took great pride in producing shapely, rounded balls of soil that were firm and well-balanced.

Periodically, I'd haul my plants to the top of the field, where another worker would come by regularly to collect and deliver them to the packing sheds. The orders were tagged with the appropriate labels, providing all the information the packers needed to send the plants on to their new homes. I used to wonder sometimes, as I crouched near the ground sculpting one of my root balls, how my plants would fare once they reached their destinations. The customers' names and addresses on the labels never failed to interest me; occasionally, I was downright fascinated. Like the time I lifted several different chestnut

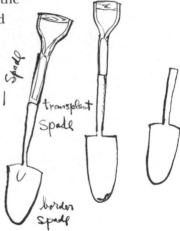

species—the genus *Castanea*—that were going to a research institute in Japan. I assumed that scientists there were attempting to develop a chestnut tree for the United States, that might someday replace our native species, which was wiped out in the early twentieth century, by a devastating blight that swept through the country's eastern deciduous forests. And the day I attached a dark blue label to one tiny pawpaw sapling (*Asimina triloba*), it delighted me no end to think that a Mrs. Graves in Lancashire might someday harvest the peculiar, sweet pulpy fruit of an American tree I knew and loved from the Blue Ridge Mountains back home. More than once I lifted plants that were bound for Sandringham Castle, one of the Queen Mother's homes, and I would imagine my plants flourishing there, pleasuring the eyes of royalty.

On rainy days during the lifting season I was sent to one of the packing sheds to work. The sheds were damp and drafty, but the job of packing plants for shipping was rather fun, and it was good to be inside for a change and enjoy the camaraderie of other students. One day I was working with two young English women, Karen and Caroline, both of whom I was fond of and who appeared to be the best of friends; those two stuck together like glue and were always giggling and whispering conspiratorially. At one point, feeling quite chilly, I left the packing table and wandered over to a big space heater a few feet away to warm up some. And as I did so, I said, "Y'all are gonna have to excuse me for a minute, but I've got to get over here and warm my fanny." Well, you've never in your life seen anything like what followed: those two women immediately collapsed into uncontrollable fits of laughter. I thought they were going to fall on the floor and die. They simply could not compose themselves. I thought, What in this world is going on? I stood there flabbergasted for the longest time, until they pulled themselves together, dried their tears, and, to my embarrassment, reluctantly informed me that "fanny" was English slang for vagina. Oops. I don't have one of those.

A couple of weeks before I was to leave Hillier's and return to the United States, I gathered a few friends together for a going-away dinner. I had recently left the hostel and moved into a cottage with three other students, so I had a place in which to entertain. I decided to call my little soirée a "Salad Party," and I sent out invitations that said "You are cordially invited to partake..." or something equally goofy.

A few days later, my brother flew over from South Carolina, and we rented a car and drove round the country. One day I got us rather stuck in a roundabout near Brighton. Later, I rammed the car into a concrete wall in a parking lot. My brother was not amused. But I was amused one day, when he tried to order an iced tea in a Burger King and the English girl behind the counter looked at him like he was crazy. "I don't see why I can't get iced tea," he muttered as we left the restaurant. One night in a London hotel room, he became convinced that somebody was loitering just outside our door, waiting to attack us upon exiting. Able to stand it no longer, and dangerously on the verge of joining him in his paranoia, I yanked opened the door to a hallway full of plain air. We both had a good laugh over that one.

When I first got back home, I went around saying "the States" and "load of rubbish" and "do you fancy" this or that, 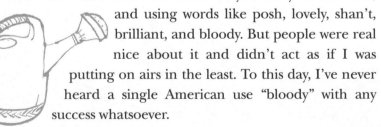 and using words like posh, lovely, shan't, brilliant, and bloody. But people were real nice about it and didn't act as if I was putting on airs in the least. To this day, I've never heard a single American use "bloody" with any success whatsoever.

3. roots

TEN YEARS AGO I LIVED briefly in a dank, one-room shack with a broken shower and no commode, in Woodstock, New York. I was up from Brooklyn, where I still had an apartment, for my second season in the Catskills. The place had a musty odor that was impossible to eradicate, but it came with a bed and the rent was dirt cheap. I peed outside under some hemlock trees and pooped in an outhouse round the corner. I didn't really mind roughing it—it was summertime and I spent virtually all my waking hours outside, working my tail off, making gardens, and building stone walls for other people. I was healthy and fed and grateful for a roof over my head, but at thirty-four years old I wanted a house with a real bathroom. And I was good and ready for a place to put down country roots, have a cookout

53

for friends, and grow a garden of my very own. Besides, I was used to a flush toilet.

Every Thursday, like clockwork, I bought the new *Woodstock Times* to see what was for rent. Every Thursday I was disappointed—nothing seemed affordable. One Saturday in mid-July I was invited to lunch at my friend Kate's, but I got there late.  Why? Because I went first to the Hudson Valley Mall in Kingston, parked in front of JC Penney's, sat in my pickup truck, and cried about my housing situation. I finally pulled myself together when an old lady with a kind face, who was getting into the car next to mine, saw me leaning my head against the steering wheel and asked if I was all right. When I looked up at her and answered that I merely had a "slight personal problem," she smiled sweetly and said, "You're a big boy, look on the bright side of things." I thanked her but sat there wondering, What bright side? Her face, something in me answered. I started my truck and drove back to Woodstock to have lunch with my friend.

The next week I bought the paper as usual and flipped to the back section. The following ad leapt from the page: "Two bedroom bungalow, screened porch, privacy, mountain views. $300 per month." I was on the phone lickety-split. The landlady answered, said the house was still available, and agreed to show it to me later that day. As I drove out of Woodstock to meet the woman, I found myself driving along the beautiful Esopus Creek—which qualifies as a small river in my book—and eventually passed through the tiny hamlet of Phoenicia, about twenty-five miles west of Woodstock. I had been there before and was once again struck by its authentic, small-town charm. It totally lacked the carnival atmosphere and gimmicky look of Woodstock, a place where hordes of tourists wander the streets in summer, looking like disappointed people in an amusement park.

A few minutes later I arrived at the woman's house, introduced myself, and followed her in my truck as she drove a short distance away. When we turned into the drive and approached the bungalow, my heart sank a bit because smack-dab beside it was another house just like it. Where does the "privacy" part come in? I wondered. Keep an open mind, I told myself, as I got out of my truck and walked with the landlady across the yard.

I soon forgot the nearness of the neighbor, because the moment I stepped onto the screened front porch, the floor

under my feet felt good. I walked to the far end to find a picturesque view of green mountains rising up all around. Stretching away from the house for perhaps a hundred feet was a flat, grassy yard in full sun, with nothing in it but a big lilac bush. The yard rolled out to a lush meadow filled with tall wildflowers—asters, goldenrod, and joe-pye weed—on the verge of bursting into bloom. The only manmade objects in sight were a sweet little wooden shed, which clearly came with the house, and a rubber tire planter sitting to one side of it. There's your privacy, I thought, as I gazed across the shimmering valley. And as I looked approvingly at the yard, I knew I was seeing one of the prettiest garden spots I'd ever laid eyes on.

Moments later, I stepped from the porch and into a small living room, which had a big window that featured the same irresistible view. A pair of tiny bedrooms lay directly in front of me like two peas in a pod. When I turned my head to the right and saw a small kitchen with an old-fashioned porcelain sink, I knew I was home. The funny blue bathroom had a working commode.

I slept in the house for the first time three nights later. As I snuggled into bed, a smile spread over my face that almost turned to laughter. I had spent the last ten years bouncing around the country, from Nantucket Island to Atlanta to San Francisco to New York City, and back again. Now I felt at home. I've been here for a decade now and I can say with total honesty that I could not be happier in a mansion filled with gold. It's never bothered me for a thin second that I don't own this house—I often say you can't take anything with you when the trumpets blow. Possessions are overrated.

Partly due to financial constraints and partly due to having my eyes wide open, I've learned how to be utterly happy with very little and lately discovered that I need even less. The religion of materialism that rules our culture distresses me; the detritus of modern life turns my stomach.

My house is funky to say the least, with sagging floors, a few cracks in the walls, and a groundhog living underneath. But the warm light that streams through my windows and suffuses the rooms of this house moves me indescribably, and it doesn't cost me an extra nickel. When I step onto my porch on a chilly evening and catch the moon on the rise, I feel like the luckiest human being alive. Nothing comforts me more than to stand at my kitchen sink washing dishes and reflecting on the day that's gone before. My home has become a gathering place for my friends. When we dine on my porch in summer, and the creek nearby tumbles and sings through the valley, there is no better place in this world.

Sticks and Stones

IF YOU HAD TOLD ME twenty years ago, when I was a young horticulture student, that my own first garden would be rectangular in shape, laid out in a formal design, and enclosed by a homemade stick fence, I would have thought you were touched in the head. Had you gone on to predict that in it would grow petunias, sunflowers, and zinnias, I would have laughed my head off and asked you kindly to gather your wits. But had you been so bold as to suggest that my future garden would include beanpoles, a birdbath, and a rubber tire planter, I would have lost my sense of humor, called you feebleminded, and pitched a fit.

I was a terrible plant snob back then, had no interest whatsoever in formal garden design, and thought vegetables were something I'd maybe get around to in my old age. I thought annual flowers, not to mention birdbaths, were totally frivolous—things to amuse and occupy little old ladies. When I began horticulture school I went from not knowing any Latin names to knowing dozens and dozens practically overnight. Suddenly I could not abide common names. I suppose this was just part of becoming a professional (and being young), but I'm glad that phase is long over.

Now I love common names—the more country and colloquial the better—and use them every chance I get. Who can resist corn cockles, baby blue eyes, or love-in-a-puff? And a pretty spring flower called "honesty" is just fine by me. Common names are evocative, colorful, and often poetic. Forsythia is one of my least favorite plants on the globe, so when I want to have a better attitude about it I use my mother's name for it—yellowbells—and I am instantly reminded of her funeral, on a sad-happy day in March, when yellowbell bushes flowered to beat the band, everywhere I looked.

I imagined my first garden would be more like a botanical collection of native trees, shrubs, and herbaceous wildflowers. Banished from this garden would have been all variegated foliage, large, showy flowers, and improved (hybridized) perennials of any kind. I pictured my plants growing in a wooded setting with rustic paths winding through it. I saw acres of deciduous azaleas, stewartias, various species of maple and magnolia, sourwood trees and Franklinias, and hundreds of orchids and trilliums. I didn't see one straight line, and neither a place to sit nor a speck of ornamentation anywhere. Who knows, perhaps I'll have such a naturalistic garden someday—I still like my fantasy image. But guess what. . . .

My first garden, which I still have today and whose plantings change every year, turned out to be filled with string beans and sunflowers, tall zinnias in a mix of colors like a handful of jellybeans, eggplants and four-o'clocks, lettuce and beets, hot marigolds, bright blue cornflowers, and jazzy gazanias. And smack in the middle of the whole crazy shooting match, spilling madly from a rubber tire planter, were outrageous striped petunias. Whoa, Nelly! Put on the brakes! How did that happen?

I'll get to that in good time, but for now, here's a description (laced with a bit of commentary by yours truly) that accompanies a full-page photograph taken in August of that first year and featured in a book by Sir Roy Strong called *Successful Small Gardens:* "This tiny potager, like an oasis in a wilderness, has an almost hallucinatory quality [well said], yet its ingredients could not be more modest [why, thank you, Sir Roy]. The area is enclosed by rustic palings in keeping with natural surroundings [precisely], but which are also functional in keeping hungry rabbits out [oh really?]. Inside, it is symmetrically divided and the cobble-edged beds are jammed with an inspiring mixture of edible and ornamental plants. Towering sunflowers, runner bean pyramids and massed nasturtiums blur the boundaries between useful and decorative kitchen garden plants. Flowers like nicotiana, cleome and cosmos are there purely for decoration, but the scattering of French marigolds in the beds helps deter pests [maybe]. Every aspect of the planting patently gives pleasure [that depends on my mood], from the gone-to-seed grasses [try radishes in flower] to the glossy leaves of the ruby chard, but the garden is obviously productive and practical [indeed]."

Allow me to say how flattered and delighted I am to have my garden included in a book by Roy Strong, one of England's foremost garden historians and a noted gardener himself. His description is excellent for someone who never set foot in my garden. And while thoroughly perplexed as to how anyone could mistake radishes for grasses, I find this easy to forgive. But it ruffles my feathers that my garden is included in a section of the book entitled "Gardens Needing about a Day a Week." I beg your pardon? A day a week of what—rain? Certainly not work.

I spend hours in my garden almost every day of the week, from March until December. If I only spent one day a week in my garden, it would quickly become a ragged, weedy mess and I would soon be institutionalized for insanity. Had the book publisher bothered to ring me, I could've easily cleared up the radish gaffe and would've proudly informed him that I virtually live in my garden. I may not be digging and planting every second, but there is more to gardening than mere backbreaking labor—that's the easy part. I happen to feel that my plantings, while never perfect, have improved dramatically over the years. I spend countless hours in my garden doing nothing but observing it in detail, painting pictures in my mind of flawless plantings that I convince myself, year after year, I can achieve. All of my gardens occupy every nook and cranny of my brain, 365 days a year. Now there's a nice chapter heading for a book on successful gardens: "Gardens Requiring 24–7."

There is something to be said for low-maintenance gardening. Not everyone wants to, or can, devote his whole life to this endeavor, and yet everyone who wishes to have a garden should have one, or spend time in somebody else's, or pass by one on the way to work each day. Unfortunately, most of the chatter about low-maintenance gardening is a lot of windy talk: very few gardens in their seasons don't require at least a constant eagle eye, if not daily hands-on work. And for those who are utterly consumed by gardening, it is no more a pastime or hobby than singing was for Maria Callas or painting for Picasso. There are people in this world, I among them, who are never, in a sense, free of their gardens. For us, gardening, though lots of fun at times, is a dead-serious business—our art, on which we spend most of our money and for which we relinquish all other pursuits.

I'm reading an excellent book at the moment called *Color by Design*, by Nori and Sandra Pope, who live and garden in Somerset, England. Theirs is one of the top ten gardens in the world that I am dying to see in the flesh. They are cutting-edge colorists who liken their work in a most thrilling way to painting and musical composition. (I wonder what they would think of my three-ring circus of color.) But here is what brings me to the Popes: In the introduction, they state that their book is about "the pursuit of gardening as a means of expression. Our garden is an accurate reflection of ourselves, and of how we interface with the natural world; it is intensely entangled with our aesthetic lives. In no way is our garden a low-maintenance or frugal affair." Bravo! I hear you loud and clear—let's go for drinks! I want to jump up and down and go over the moon when I know other people in the world feel this way.

I don't know anymore where my garden stops and I begin—it's all too down deep in my bones. We are one. When I finally got to make a garden of my own, I went around in a state of euphoria for ages. I managed to be still when I had to ride on a train or drive in my car, but some nights I tossed and turned like a child on Christmas Eve. I still lived in New York City part-time, and when I went out to dinner, I tried to turn almost any conversation to beets and sunflowers or matters of soil. My friends were all quite good about it, but I'm sure I was unbearable. When the time came each week to go back to the country, I'd be fine until I got a mile from my driveway, when I'd want to jump out of my skin to get home faster and see my garden.

To this day, when I arrive home from almost anywhere—unless it's pouring down rain or the yard is full of snow, and even when I have to pee, because one of the great joys of living in the country is whipping it out wherever—I take the long way around to enter the house, by first walking through the garden. And unless I'm in a big hurry when I leave home to go somewhere, I take the long way around again, before getting in my car, so I can say good-bye to my garden in case I die in a car wreck.

The day I started tilling the soil for my new garden and removing rocks and weeds from the earth, I felt like my soul was guzzling water after a long time in the desert. I had not been unhappy during the foregoing years, but I simply hadn't known what I was missing. I knew something inside of me was asleep, trying to wake up and live and grow, kick up its heels and dance. And I knew, of course, that it would have something to do with plants and gardens—I just didn't know when or where it would happen or how it would manifest itself.

But I will tell you the truth: for a couple of years before I finally found my place in the country, a vague image began to appear in my mind of a small cottage with a fenced garden and a wonderful front porch. The reality looks a lot like the mental picture I used to carry around—no lie. When I was making my first garden I felt something was being born that already existed. I felt like a sculptor, though I've never used a chisel in my life. I was eagerly peeling away layers, and that is why I couldn't shut up when I was dining out in New York, about the beets and sunflowers I was going to grow, just you wait and see.

I started making my garden a few weeks after I moved into my house in the Catskills. On a day in late September, I picked up a ball of twine, a sack of white flour, a hammer, a tape measure, and a handful of small wooden stakes, walked out into the grassy yard on the private side of my house, where the meadow was golden and purple and mauve and the mountains nearby were beginning to burn with autumn color, paced around for a while, and proceeded to do the only remotely arbitrary thing of major importance I would do in the making of my garden: without considering for a second how I would fit a sensible configuration of beds and paths into its dimensions, I measured a rectangle 22 feet by 30 feet, simply because it looked right, pounded stakes into the ground at each corner, ran twine along the entire perimeter, outlined it with white flour and stood back and looked at the embryo of my garden.

For days I worked like a dog, rototilling the entire plot, removing stones and perennial weeds as I went. I'd drop to the ground periodically to rest and just sit there running the soil through my hands like it was gold (it's better than gold), gazing at the mountains, knowing I was the same as everything around me, seeing the sky and thinking about the center of the earth and the age of the universe and why things and life are the way they are, feeling my heartbeat and the sweat on my skin and the electricity in the air.

I used an old tiller I had bought with a friend for a hundred bucks (it wasn't worth fifty) that almost shook me to death, jumping like crazy through the rocky earth, and after I finished with that poor contraption it never saw another day's work. My soil is full of smooth, rounded stones, but once they come out, its texture is lovely and loamy and it smells better than anything I can name. As I worked, I piled mounds of stone along the perimeter of the garden—it looked as if some strange ceremony were about to take place. My old friend Ron, from Nantucket, came for a visit during that time, and one day he helped me load them into the bed of my truck, haul them to the meadow, and toss them away. But the largest and shapeliest ones I put aside for later use.

In October the mountains blazed gloriously. Everybody said it was the prettiest fall they had seen here in years. Most days I'd work in the garden almost till dark, or until my bones told me to stop, then I'd run inside and get a glass of wine or a cold beer and go right back outside. I had an old cinderblock I'd position near the house, smack in front of the garden, where I could sit down, lean back, and rest my weary body while admiring the day's progress. My belly would growl from hunger and my hands would be chilly and raw, but I'd be in absolute heaven, gazing into the garden, where I could see myself watering sprouts and touching leaves, smelling flowers and tending my beds, planting things with my hands and breathing the sweet, fresh air.

When the last piece of light had faded from the world, I'd go inside and fix a little supper, and no matter what it was, I'd feel utterly grateful. My chin would drop to my chest, and I'd run through all the blessings in my life, while I thought about a world where some people have far too much and most have little or nothing, and I would ask myself, How did you get so lucky as to have a house to shelter you, a piece of earth to a grow a garden in, and so many people in your life to love? Had you found me dead in my bed during that time I would have had a smile on my face, because life doesn't get any better.

Most nights I got into bed with a sketch pad, a pile of garden books, and a journal in which I jotted down ideas. I devoured Page's book, *The Education of a Gardener*. Page was born in England in 1906 and became the international garden designer of our time, working throughout England, Europe, and the United States. Heavily influenced by the French classical period and blessed with impeccable taste, he was a master of scale and proportion and a plantsman of the first order. His gardens were the epitome of style and sophistication, and like many a great artist, he strove, in the end, for simplicity. My favorite three sentences from his book can be found in a chapter called "Sites and Themes": "The problem for the garden maker is always the same, and I always try to discover in what consists the significance of the site, and then base my garden theme on that. For a theme of some kind, a basic idea, is essential. It will set the rhythm of your composition down to its smallest details."

When those sentences entered my eyes, I read them over and over. I was already onto my "basic idea" of a flower and vegetable patch, a kitchen garden, what everybody today just loves to run around calling a potager. And I knew I was going to build a stick fence and use stones to edge my beds. "Significance of the site" and "rhythm of your composition" jumped from the page like writing on the wall. Russell Page was speaking about a broad approach to landscape, but his philosophy applied equally to my small plot of ground. No wonder sticks and stones felt so right to me: these simple native materials I was planning to use to structure and frame my garden would respect the deciduous landscape of the Catskills perfectly. Not only that, sticks and stones would cost me nothing, which was a good thing, since I was broke. Not that I ever for a moment considered a store-bought fence.

Three major things influenced my decision to make a kitchen garden: first, during my years as a waiter, and partic- ularly while working at Zuñi Café, in San Francisco—where Judy Rogers turns out some of the best food in California—I had come to appreciate simple, fresh fare made with great ingredients; second, for a short time while living in Atlanta, I had worked for garden designer Ryan Gainey, whose charming, walled vegetable garden knocked me off my feet with its diamond-shaped beds, box edging, and intimate feeling of enclosure; and third, the previous spring I had planted the first vegetable garden of my life, for my friend and client, Kate Pierson, in Woodstock. I was hooked.

In Kate's garden we had mixed flowers and vegetables in raised beds, so I had seen the practicality and beauty in this. But the beds, laid out by someone else, were very oddly shaped—a rambling affair with no geometric pattern or sensible rhythm at all. The garden's rustic cedar fence, built by my friend William, featured a lovely steeped arbor and woven-twig gate at the entrance. A small flight of steps he made at the rear of the garden were beautifully constructed of native stone and lead into the adjacent woods. But the space inside was most unsatisfactory and impossible to plant well. Two years later, to keep from pulling my hair out, I threw myself into a massive overhaul, creating a simple grid of raised beds and narrow paths, which maximized the growing area and changed my life in that garden. It is absolutely amazing what organization can do for a vegetable garden, not to mention for one's state of mind.

For inspiration in designing my garden I turned repeatedly to Rosemary Verey's book, *Classic Garden Design,* where I found loads of practical advice on making a decorative kitchen garden. I had long admired pictures of her potager at Barnsley House, in Gloucestershire, with its intricacy, its tapestry of plants, and the orderly calm that appeared to pervade this colorful, textured world. I wanted it bad. Was it possible to have such a garden in my own life?

Quite soon, using plain white paper and an architect's scale, I designed a garden that would consist of twelve beds, which I grouped and named: the Entrance (a double gate and two small beds either side of it), the Outer Quads (four large beds—two on each side—stretching the length of the fence), the Rear Border (a focal point through the main axis), and the Inner Garden (a small circular bed at the center and four rectangular beds around it). Except for the one at the center, all beds would be 4 feet across; side paths would measure 18 inches wide, and the cross axes would be slightly wider at 24 inches.

It was thrilling to see my formal garden in miniature and think of carving its geometry into the earth. I carried my plan around with me and showed it off to friends because I had never before drawn anything satisfactorily on paper. And by the way, my design fitted perfectly the rectangle I had already made in the yard, and I didn't have to fudge in the least.

The idea for my fence came from Deborah and Patrick, good friends from horticulture school in North Carolina who had moved to Virginia and bought land in the country while I was living in England. On my first trip to visit them in their new home, not long after I had moved to Atlanta, I saw a stick fence Patrick made to go around their vegetable patch; I was charmed right down to my toes and knew I wanted one someday.

Their garden was set on a hilltop with a view that stretched for miles across a gentle, mountainous valley. When I stepped inside I felt protected by and held in the hands of the garden. I had the sense of being in a small, private world that was still connected to the larger landscape, like the secure feeling I get when looking out a window of my house. It was during that visit that I came out to Deborah and Patrick. It occurs to me now that the safety and happiness I felt in their garden is metaphorical of the acceptance and love my friends expressed when I told them that weekend that I was gay. And it strikes me as perfect that the sight of their beautiful handmade fence planted a seed in my mind for my future garden.

By late October I had finished tilling the soil and it was time to begin my fence. But I had never built anything that didn't involve Tinker Toys or Lincoln Logs, and that had been a while. In the weeks before I started building, I observed every picket fence I came upon, and browsed through books to find examples. I noted over and over how the rails attached to the outside of posts, and the pickets to the outside of rails, and recorded in my mind the balanced placement of all the components. I did this with all the concentration of someone trying to understand rocket science or brain surgery I am a person born to dig holes and grow plants, but my building skills are rudimentary to say the least—pathetic, really. The more I thought about my fence, however, the more I knew I could, should, and would build it.

My landlord owns a lumber mill nearby, where he allowed me to pick through piles of discarded wood. I found plenty of weathered gray posts, and pine 1 x 4's to use as rails. I had a good old time rummaging through and making my selections. As I trudged back and forth through the meadow, hauling my booty home, I basked in the autumn beauty of the Catskills. I had decided the fence would be $4\frac{1}{2}$ feet tall, which would be in good scale with the beds inside the garden. I borrowed a post-hole digger from a friend and worked my way methodically round the garden, digging a hole, planting a post, digging a hole, planting a post. (This took several days: for each of the fourteen posts I dug an 18-inch hole through layers of stone.) I cut the posts to the appropriate length with a dull pruning saw—talk about a workout!—but buying a new saw was an extravagance that I could not afford. Once the posts were up and the soil was packed firmly around them, I made quick work of attaching the rails with nails. The garden already felt like a room, a haven—and I had made it with my own bare hands.

One afternoon I grabbed my twine, tape measure, wooden stakes, and a half-moon edging tool, pinned my plan to the wall of the house, and proceeded to lay out the beds. If I were to explain in detail how I did this, it would read like a complicated instruction manual for doing something simple. Essentially, I created a template for the garden at ground level by tying the twine to the wooden stakes (this involved much running back and forth to consult my plan). When I was finished, the crisscrossing twine looked like a maze, but I could discern the design I had drawn on paper. Next, I used the edging tool to cut the beds into the soil as precisely and carefully as I possibly could. When I removed the twine and stakes, the geometry of the garden emerged. A plain rectangle of tilled earth had suddenly become a work of art.

Over the next few weeks, as the weather turned cold and the days shortened, I walked

half moon edger

on the paths of the garden constantly, packing them down and smoothing their surfaces, while imagining how I would plant the beds come spring. It is not an overstatement in the least to say that this was a major turning point in my life. My eyes could not get enough of what I had done. It was very exciting to see this piece of ground changed into an intricate world where form and symmetry prevailed. My simple four-square garden was nothing more than a variation on a theme, a new interpretation of an ancient design—perhaps the most copied, basic garden plan in history. But there wasn't another one like mine in the world. It was original, yet related to other gardens in the past and present by virtue of its classic lines.

During this time I kept looking at the rubber tire planter sitting beside my shed that had been there since the day I moved in. No! No! No! I thought, over and over, You are not going to use it. But one day I picked that sucker up and plopped it down in the circular bed in the middle of the garden and it's never moved since.

By Thanksgiving the ground in my garden was wet and cold and I stopped working for the season. I invited my friends Cal and Ken for the holiday, and roasted my first turkey, using a recipe I found in a cookbook from the Phoenicia library, which called for wrapping the bird in cheesecloth soaked with tons of butter. That was the best turkey I've ever put in my mouth, before or since. With it we had greens and potatoes, cornbread stuffing, cranberry something-or-other, and pumpkin pie for desert. We had the most festive time in the world, drinking wine and lounging on a $10 couch I had bought at a yard sale, while laughing about the ugly refrigerator sitting in the corner of my living room (it eventually moved to the porch).

My friends were delighted to see the tire planter sitting grandly at the center of my garden. On a previous visit they had dissuaded me from hauling it to the dump, where I was sure it belonged. "Y'all know, as well as I do, that thing is tacky as all get out—I'm not about to put it in my new garden," I stated flatly. "Child, you have got to use it, it just goes here," they insisted. And it does, it just goes here. It's perfect for my funky shack and modest garden and the right size for its situation. I must have known my friends were right all along, because one day right before Thanksgiving, I found myself thinking about my rusty pickup truck, the trailers up and down my road, and the refrigerator in my living room. That's when I said, Get over it, Dean—context is everything. In seconds flat I hauled the tire planter to its rightful place, where it has ruled supreme for ten years.

As tire planters go, mine is particularly shapely and well-crafted. The flared, zigzag edge, which appears to have been fashioned with a giant pair of pinking shears, is beautifully executed. I wonder who made it and how it came to be in my yard? It turns out to be an excellent container for growing plants; perhaps the black rubber absorbs and holds heat without drying the roots too much. All I know is that I rarely have to hand-water it, even in dry weather. When my parents were in my garden my mother asked me what it was. "Mama, that's nothing but a car tire turned inside out, sitting on its hub. I know you've seen at least a million of them back home." "Dean, honey, I declare," she said, amazed.

The first winter in my new home was mild and there was

very little snow. The occasional dusting left a painterly touch on the garden and lifted the geometry of the beds into bold relief. It was nice to stand at the window and look directly into the garden, while dreaming of finishing my fence. But I had given little thought to where I would get all the sticks I was going to need. Luckily, road maintenance crews began clearing growth from nearby roadsides, and neat piles of saplings appeared everywhere.

And what a godsend they turned out to be. On my days up from the city, I'd jump in my truck with loppers and a saw and go collecting. Somehow all those free sticks seemed too good to be true; I always expected some cop to pull over and ruin my fun by telling me I was breaking the law. Most of the sticks were ash, oak, hickory, and maple. Right away, I grew partial to ash—its stems were almost straight and its bark was smooth and unblemished. The wood looked as if it would take a nail easily (it does), and I knew baseball bats were made of ash, so I figured it would be quite durable (it is). No cop ever busted me and my shed was soon filled with hundreds of sticks.

In early March I began the last phase of fence building. I'll never forget the morning I flounced into the yard, threw open the shed door with a vengeance, and grabbed about 200 sticks, fully intending to nail every one to the rails by sundown. When I had the first few in place, I stood back to assess my progress: You *crazy* queen! I thought. What on earth have you let yourself in for? It was painfully clear I had miles left to go: 104 linear feet of fence doesn't look like much until you start moving along it at a snail's pace, cutting more than 500 sticks to size and attaching them 4 inches apart. And when you hold a round stick against a flat rail and try to marry the two with a nail, the stick just loves to roll around and misbehave. I got faster with practice, and my carpentry steadily improved, but it still took weeks to finish.

I was often forced to take breaks and go inside to nurse my left thumb, which I regularly bludgeoned with a hammer. And once a week I had to stop and go to the city for three days to be a waiter, where I yapped and yapped about my fence to whoever would listen. When it was finished, I thought it was the finest structure I had ever seen. I was also amazed that it didn't collapse. In fact, it didn't even wobble.

In April the sun got warm and sassy and tried to chase old winter away (it never really scrams around here till about June 1). Red maples flushed with color and fleecy white

shadbush dotted the landscape. Robins and catbirds pranced about like snappy people at a fun party, and the days got long and pretty. Silvery pussy willows woke in the wet meadow and dressed in cotton-fresh fluff. A batch of barn swallows fussed and twittered in my roof eaves, and rabbits nibbled in the yard. Blackbirds dipped and dove in the sky, the stream nearby rushed and jumped through the valley, and children yelped and played till dark. By the end of the month, fresh green was creeping up the mountainsides, the grass was spangled with dandelions, and I was lunching on my porch every day. In the garden, I pounced on every sorry weed I saw. Some peas I'd pushed in the ground on April 1 popped their necks up, just like that. I thought, Spring is here for sure!

My landlord offered me all the horse manure I wanted out of his barn. Girl, I hit the jackpot! That stuff was black and rich. I made at least fifteen trips over there in my truck to fill a big barrel, over and over, and soon had a mountain of manure sitting by the shed. Next I spread gobs and gobs of it on every bed in the garden and worked it deeply into the soil with a spading fork. One day my neighbor dropped by with a friend to show her the garden. I sprang at the women with a fat chunk of the beautiful manure in my hands, to show it off and share my excitement. The friend, who had an elaborate, mesmerizing hairdo and a face caked with makeup, was a sight to behold, backing away from me, staring unblinkingly, ready to run for her life. I thought, Get a grip, Dean. It's just some good doo-doo.

When the manure was used up, I smoothed the beds nicely with a steel rake, and started edging them with cobblestones. I had a few that had come from the soil when I tilled it back in October; the rest I gathered by the stream across the road. I've never counted how many stones it finally took, but I'd guess it to be about 400.

In early May I commenced planting. I had no idea what I was doing. I was thrilled with my new garden but overwhelmed by the design. The only thing I knew for sure was that I wanted a framework of shrubs in the Rear Border. I splurged at a local nursery on a tree hydrangea, a sand cherry, a rose, a spiraea, and a 2-gallon pot of zebra grass. These formed the backbone of the Rear Border and almost emptied my sad pockets—all other plants would have to be cheap. From then on, I bought whatever seeds struck my fancy and the best dime-store annuals I could lay my hands on, and I planted that garden to beat the band.

I filled in around the shrubs with tall white tobacco, white cleome, State Fair zinnias, and dark blue cornflowers. In the Outer Quads I made stick pyramids and planted them with scarlet runner beans. I filled the tire planter with Crimson Star petunias and lined the fence with Heavenly Blue morning glories. Some days I felt formal and some days I felt natural. I made rows and blocks, circles and blobs, groups of one and groups of ten. I put lettuce to the left and beets to the right, poppies here and cosmos there. One day I felt like chard, the next like spinach, but I always felt like a sunflower. I fussed and picked and fretted and puzzled and was on that garden like white on rice.

My neighbor's little boy, Josh, said, "You're always on your work." He loved to help me, so I'd sprinkle a few nasturtium seeds in his hands and he'd plant them wherever he wished.

After about two minutes, he'd be dying to water—that was his favorite job. So I'd let him slosh around for a while and make a mess, even if the sky was about to rain. He asked me once if I was growing any mozzarella or parmesan in the garden. I thought, Lord, have mercy, child.

By late May I had every square inch of the garden planted. On Memorial Day weekend I stopped at a yard sale down the road, where, for $25, I bought a fantastic pair of con-crete urns, adorned on their sides with porcelain faces of cats and ladies. They were the perfect orna-ments to mark my garden's entrance. I dubbed them the cat-lady urns. To me, they are peer-less: I wouldn't sell them today for $1,000, not if you chased me down the road with a checkbook. (That's a good feeling.)

Later that week I saw a sign by somebody's driveway that said "Free Stuff," and sitting there like magic was a fine Adirondack chair. When I plopped that boy down at one end of the garden's cross path, with a kingly view of the tire planter, it fit like a glove. A few weeks later, at a salvage yard, I bought a plain, concrete birdbath, chipped and scarred just right, to go at the other end of the cross path. (Don't you know I wanted to die when the first bird stopped by for a dip and a sip?) These three simple fea-tures—urns, chair, and birdbath—along with the tire planter, are still the only ornaments in the fenced garden.

In the decoration department, give me simplicity and understatement or give me nothing.

Every night I flopped into bed thinking surely nothing would grow, and every morning I changed my mind. I'd sit up in bed, scoot to the window, and look out at the garden, and for a few seconds—a few pure seconds—everything was brand new. Summer was wet and cool and as green as could be—black-green on the mountains. I was always waking up at night to the sound and smell of rain. (Once, when there was a full moon in a clear sky, I woke to a loud munching sound. I got up, walked to the other bedroom window, and just about dropped my teeth: 10 feet away, in the silver-blue night was a white horse with brown spots, grazing in my yard. I stood there with my mouth open, trying to form a word for nobody in the room. But that's another story, and it has a sad ending, so let's leave off in the moonlight.) In the mornings, the sun slid from the meadow and into the garden, touched the growing sprouts, and made them glisten and glow. On days when the sun played hooky, it was fine with me—I like all kinds of weather. The garden grew and grew. No, the garden exploded.

For a few weeks, my eyes knew every seedling and each new branch and blossom. Then suddenly, in July, the ground was covered. Thousands of leaves were touching each other and lovely flowers of every color—living in my own garden!—bloomed everywhere. I tried to keep up, but could not. The great crescendo came in August, when the State Fair zinnias crashed onto the stage and pushed everybody aside with their loud blossoms of pink, orange, yellow, and red. One sunflower shot to 13 feet and got a stem on it the size of a man's ankle. Some blue morning glories on the fence nearby said, *Look out! Here we come!* and leapt onto the giant sunflower and scrambled to the top of its golden, blossoming head. I have to say it—that garden was a picture. Before it was all over, crickets jumped in from the meadow, set up shop in the Rear Border, and carried on like they owned the place. That did it—I was a basket case.

Around the time of the crickets, the musical band, the B-52s, made a video in my yard. I thought my garden was going to be the star of the show; otherwise I wouldn't have allowed them to take over my life for 14 hours. But before I tell the story, here are two things to remember: If a video director with a big-time band ever asks to shoot in your yard, say no, absolutely not. If you spinelessly break down, and say yes, demand way more money than what they offer, and stand your ground when they squirm and whine, because they've got cash to burn, and don't you believe otherwise.

They must have, because they can afford to pay seven people to sit around in lawn chairs and read paperback books, while another thirteen walk around in circles. Once in a while, one of these twenty will get bored and join the eight or nine people standing in line to use your phone. (This was before cell phones became attached to every other ear in the world.) The remaining forty-one humans stay very busy, eating and drinking. Oh, I almost forgot— the cameraman films the band, the director frets about everything, and the sexy producer with the goatee runs around in a flimsy pair of shorts, flirting with the owner of the yard (I didn't mind that part).

None of my ranting has anything whatsoever to do with my friend Kate, who's in the band, or any of the other members. I was the fool who flapped his jaws to begin with, when she mentioned to me that the director was scouting for a scenic location. "Send him over!" I said. Of course, he loved it, because my valley is a very scenic location. And how could he possibly resist my nice flat yard? After all, he needed a place where all those important people could sit down and read. I just wish I had known to extract lots of money from him. I should have asked Kate to make him cough up more cash, but she was busy trying to balance the world's tallest, reddest, bouffant hairdo on top of her head.

The agreement was for them to arrive early and leave early. The first van rolled in about 7 a.m. By noon, the driveway was filled with cars and trucks, two huge buses (the band was on tour), and a Winnebago camper, which served as an office. One caterer set up tables outside, another spread food all over my porch. Suddenly, a bright green wooden stage the size of my garden appeared in my yard, exactly where a white-and-brown horse had peacefully grazed in the moonlight a few nights before. People wandered in and out of my house like it was a museum and my bathroom went into overdrive. Finally, about one o'clock, somebody got out a video camera and went to work.

Everything went along fine until my landlord, who thought some little band from Woodstock was here making a video, showed up. When he saw Fred Schneider dangling from a crane, looking like a space alien, he blew a fuse. The next thing I knew he was vanishing into the Winnebago office with the producer. When they emerged, my landlord gave me a withering look and stomped away. For weeks after that, he wouldn't wave to me when we passed each other on the road. It turns out he was afraid of being held liable if someone got hurt on his land—I didn't blame him. He also felt taken advantage of: nobody had offered him a dime. Again, I didn't blame him. Live and learn, I suppose. I'm just glad he eventually forgave me.

The last van left at 9 P.M., but not before some poor underling knocked on my porch door and asked, with a smile on his face—like he was giving me something for Christmas—if it was okay to leave five jumbo bags of garbage in my yard. I gave him three times the withering look my landlord had given me. Unfortunately, I didn't think to ask *him* if he wanted the big lime green stage sitting round the corner—perhaps because I didn't know it was still there and was mine to give away. Yippee! I sat back down with Kate and some others. We talked about the crazy day and I speculated as to whether the California producer was gay, needed a boyfriend, and wanted to move to the Catskills. Meanwhile, I was expecting company the next day. Somewhere in Pennsylvania, my parents, my brother, and my sister were checked into a motel for the night, en route from South Carolina. I was pooped and twirled and ready for bed.

My family pulled in about five o'clock the next afternoon in Daddy's new town car. And boy, was he proud of it. That fancy boat of a car looked strange parked next to my country shack. When Mama got out of "The Lincoln," as she called it, she was right giddy from the long trip, but I thought she looked so pretty. She took one look at that stupid green stage and said, "Honey, what in the land o' Goshen is that?" "Don't ask, Mama. I'll tell you later." Daddy went straight to the bathroom.

Then we all went out to the garden together. My sister Kay just said, "Oh, Mama, look." My twin brother, Gene, glanced around for a minute, smiled, and said, "Very unusual." When my mother saw the bright zinnias, her breath caught, and she looked at my father: "Lord, Henry, look here. Dean's got old maids in his garden." I said, "Mama, what are you talking about, those are zinnias." "Oh, honey, I know they are," she said, "but we always called them 'old maids' when I was a girl." And she went on to say that when she and Daddy first married, they moved to Charleston, where she planted a row of zinnias across the front of their house and thought it was the prettiest thing she'd ever seen. I bet my mother had not seen zinnias growing in a garden in many, many years. I'd give up anything in this world to go up to heaven today and present her with a fresh bouquet of them.

The next day was my brother's and my birthday. After lunch, Daddy sat at the table counting out two piles of money. What is he up to? I wondered. When he had the piles just right, he handed Gene and me $35 each, for thirty-five years. Kay took us all out to dinner at the Bear Café in Woodstock. When I ordered iced tea instead of my usual martini, Karen, the waitress, looked puzzled and asked if I was feeling well. Back at my house, we sat around talking before bedtime, and nobody acted like it was the least bit strange to see a refrigerator in a living room. Gene said, "This place suits you to a T."

On Saturday, we drove to New York City and went straight to the top of the Empire State Building, where the skies were crystal-clear. We had a hell-ride in a taxi, went to South Street Seaport, rode the subway, had lunch in a bad diner, and were driving back upstate by late afternoon. Daddy had never been to New York before, but he'd had enough—his stomach was bothering him.

They left early Monday morning to go home. Kay and Mama got misty-eyed when it was time to say good-bye. Mama said, "Honey, this was just *grand*. Now we know where you live." Daddy said, "Put something on your head in this cool weather." And off they went.

Two days later, on September 23, there was a hard frost during the night and the garden turned black and mushy. When I wrote in my journal about my folks' visit, and the garden getting frosted, I flipped back through my notes. Exactly a year before, on September 23, I had walked into my yard, marked out a rectangular plot with sticks and string, and outlined it with white flour.

Sometime before winter I took a sledgehammer, knocked that damn stage apart, and hauled it to the dump.

5. learning the ropes

OVER THE PAST TEN YEARS I've got more comfortable with the design of my fenced garden and learned how best to plant it. I call it the Main Garden now, to distinguish it from the other gardens I've made here. In the first year I didn't see the big picture clearly, didn't see the forest for the trees, which is why I went around planting a row here and a blob there. But perhaps this was a good way to learn. After all, a forest begins with a tree. I knew I had made a garden with good bones and proper scale and proportion. But the first-year plantings, much as I enjoyed them, were naïve and playful. Playful I still like. Naïve—defined as artless—wore thin very quickly. I'm actually rather embarrassed by the picture in Roy Strong's book of my first-year effort. The garden looks dotty, like something a child had planted.

Now I know to approach the garden as a single entity made of several related parts. And though I always aim for lush, colorful wildness—a garden that engulfs me in vegetation by summer's end—I also strive for simplicity and calm by remembering two key elements of good design: repetition and balance. From the beginning, when I drew the garden on paper, I divided the beds into groups and named them: Outer Quads, Inner Garden, Rear Border and Entrance. But for some reason, in the first year, I paid very little attention to this as I went about sowing seeds and digging holes wherever I pleased. Beginning in the second year, I saw I had built a garden with a life of its own and a story to tell. Ever since, I've tried to listen, play my part, and do my baby right.

It's still a garden composed almost entirely of annual flowers and vegetables. With the exception of the Rear Border and four evergreen box shrubs that mark the corners of the Inner Garden, it's newly planted each spring. This allows me a great deal of experimentation—important in all gardens, but especially so in small ones like mine. It also means a lot of work, but anything worth having is worth working for. I used to hate that adage when I was a child, but now I know it's true. I met a famous and brilliant gardener in North Carolina a few years ago and toured her fine garden. When I said something about gardening being hard work, she screeched: "Work! Work! This isn't work, this is pure pleasure!" Relax, I wanted to say, I hear you, I get it, but my aching back and cracked hands tell me it's work, too. Hard work. I wonder if she's ever built a stone wall.

Every winter I fret and puzzle about what to plant come

spring, but I never make decisions until the weather has warmed and I'm in the garden cleaning up. Actually, I don't make serious decisions until I go plant shopping in April and May. One of the good things about a simple four-square design is that you can carry the geometry of the garden around in your head when you're out browsing through nurseries and greenhouses. And though I don't plant the garden in a strictly formal manner at all, I often buy plants in multiples of four, knowing I can figure out later just where things will go. And I am talking mainly about inexpensive plants—cell packs of four or six plants at less than $2 a pop—so if I buy too many, it's no big deal. I can always give some away.

I also buy a lot of seeds—sunflowers, morning glories, nasturtiums, lettuce, arugula, chard—but only things I can sow directly in the ground or in peat pots on my porch; I have no greenhouse. I always go overboard with seeds, but so does everyone I know. There are racks upon racks of seed packets at my favorite garden center, where more than a dozen seed houses are represented. I don't think I've ever picked up a seed packet without shaking it to hear the sound the seeds make, scratching against the paper. Beet and chard seeds, nubby and rough, make a percussive, musical sound, like brushes on a snare drum. Nasturtiums are fun, too, rolling around inside their packets like tiny wooden marbles. Fine seeds like lettuce make a soft, whispery sound. Poppy seeds are tiny, so tiny they are almost silent. Beans, on the other hand, shout—particularly the large ones, like scarlet runner beans. They sound serious and no-nonsense. Plant us, they seem to say, We will grow, we promise, you won't be disappointed.

In making my plant and seed selections for the Main Garden, I consider each group of beds separately and what its particular plant palette will be. The color scheme is always hot, hot, hot—lots of red and orange and magenta. Actually, almost anything goes as long as there is a good leavening of green. Like most gardeners, I like trying new things, but I am not bent on rare plants for this particular garden. This has always been a simple garden of old-fashioned flowers and everyday vegetables and I want it to remain that way. Generally speaking, I like growing plants that are easily obtained. Besides, these days it's fairly easy to buy heirloom vegetables and exciting annuals. I do believe growers have finally got on the clue train.

In the Outer Quads—the four beds, two on either side of the garden, that run the length of the fence—I plant tall things. I always grow sunflowers, which I sow in peat pots the first week in May. These will be ready for planting out by the end of the month. I grow the kind that flower up and down the stems with lots of smallish blooms: Velvet Queen, Inca Jewels, Autumn Beauty. (The Russian Mammoth type, which has one huge blossom the size of a Frisbee way at the top of the stem, is for the birds—literally and figuratively.) I plant each sunflower seedling in a big hole with manure or compost dug in. Each quad measures 4 feet wide from the fence to the path, so I usually plant double rows and stagger the plants—six to eight sunflowers in each bed. If I lose a few to chipmunks or cutworms, I fill in with something like cosmos, cleome, or Mexican sunflower (*Tithonia rotundifolia*).

Behind the sunflowers, all along the stick fence, I sow morning glory seeds very thickly. I never knick the seeds and soak them in water, like you're supposed to do, but I always get heavy germination. When the seedlings are 3 or 4 inches tall, I thin them to stand 6 or 8 inches apart. As the sunflowers grow up and the morning glories scamper onto the fence, various tall, self-sown annuals are allowed to rise among them—green-flowered tobacco (*Nicotiana langsdorffii*), red orach (*Atriplex hortensis* 'Rubra'), and purple *Verbena bonariensis.*

The Outer Quads are punctuated by stick pyramids that link overhead with cross sticks to form simple arbors. The arbors frame the chair and basin at either end of the garden's cross axes. I adore growing scarlet runner beans to climb up the sticks, but beans want to be rotated, so in alternate years I train my tomato vines on the arbors. This makes for a nice rotation: beans, being legumes, fix nitrogen into the soil through nodules on their roots; this benefits the tomatoes the following year. It's lovely, in a tomato year, to sit in the chair under the arbor, look to either side, and see the swelling, ripening fruits close by. And it's just as lovely, in a bean year, to enjoy the flaming red bean blossoms and watch a hummingbird feast on them. It's interesting to observe people who visit my garden and see which ones sit in the chair. A child will almost invariably go directly to it and plop down, simply because it's there, I suppose. Small children seem so in tune with the moment and unafraid to be themselves.

The Inner Garden is defined by the small circular bed at the center of the garden, surrounded by four identical beds. The circular bed holds the tire planter, which is surrounded by a tiny wattle fence I make new each spring from wood I gather in the meadow by my house. It's fun work—nothing could be easier. I use stout, straight pieces of ash wood half

tire planter

an inch thick for the uprights, and thin pussy willow whips for the horizontal weavers. First, I push the ash sticks into the ground about 6 inches deep and 8 inches apart. Next, I weave the willow through the ash, a row at a time, until the fence is about 8 inches high. This simple bit of ornamentation sets the planter off and attracts attention to it. The small piece of ground beneath the tire is planted with golden creeping Jenny (*Lysimachia nummularia* 'Aurea'), a very flat perennial groundcover with electric leaves. The golden trailing stems look sweet poking through the wattle fence.

The tire planter is always a major consideration. Since it sits at the heart of the Main Garden, it simply must be fierce and ruling. In the early years, I often planted it with petunias. Once I filled it with nothing but snow-white petunias—small, single ones—and they grew into a perfect white dome. I deadheaded those plants like crazy and fed them extravagantly, as I do most annuals. One July day a heavy rainstorm came and flattened the perfect dome; suddenly it looked as if a hippopotamus had sat on it. One of the best plantings ever was a combination of purple ornamental kale, silvery *Helichrysum petiolare*, and Purple Wave petunias. The three kale plants grew into one huge, crinkled mound and the florescent petunias dotted all over it looked like candy. The trailing helichrysum wound through everything like some sugary strand of goop, tying it all together. I thought, My stars above.

One of the most striking plantings in the tire was a mass of Japanese blood grass, *Imperata cylindrica* 'Red Baron.' The late afternoon sun streaking through those fiery blades made for excellent garden drama; no matter where you put red in the garden, it will rivet the eye instantly. Two years ago I filled the tire with Bright Lights chard grown from seed sown directly in the planter. The plants had stems of pink, yellow, red, and white—on separate plants, mind you. Chard is my favorite ornamental vegetable. It looks fabulous all season. I can harvest the lower leaves continually for the table and still have a handsome plant to look at, and it's virtually pest-free in my garden. Last year I planted the tire with *Phormium* 'Apricot Queen.' Also known as New Zealand flax, this yucca-like plant has bold, spiky leaves. I'm not sure where the apricot part comes in—mine had lemon yellow leaves with green stripes, which suited me fine. I underplanted it with candy pink calibrachoa, or Million Bells, a petunia relative that spills and trails and flowers like mad. The effect was regal and wonderfully gaudy. This year I have red chard in the tire planter and it's looking just dandy so far.

The four beds surrounding the tire planter have notched edges—semicircles that together form a discontinuous ring at the center of the garden where the main paths converge and encircle the planter. I always use the same plant in each semicircle to accentuate the circular effect. One year I combined creeping White Star zinnias with the rounded, cloverlike blossoms of white gomphrena. It was marvelous. Another time I planted this area with Lady in Red salvia, a gorgeous, bushy plant that gets 3 feet tall and has vibrant scarlet spikes in abundance. I don't usually grow something so tall here, but this time it worked beautifully; it was fun to stand at the center of the garden inside a circle of intense red flowers. Another year I chose silvery Powis Castle artemisia, a vigorous, sprawling perennial that I treat as an annual in my zone 5 garden. It created a dreamy effect of hazy light at the heart of the garden. This year I planted a short ornamental grass, Elijah Blue fescue, for a cool, ghostly effect.

I plant the four beds in the Inner Garden in one of two ways: in long rows for a formal effect, or as tapestry plantings for an informal effect. I choose a basic plant palette and stick with it. But to give each bed its own unique look, I vary the arrangement in each one, especially when creating a tapestry planting. In both cases I use low-growing vegetables and flowers with contrasting colors, textures, and habits. In any case, I'm striving for a carpet effect, to complement the Outer Quads, the Rear Border, and the Entrance beds, whose towering plants act as living walls around the edges of the carpet.

One year in early April, I planted the Inner Garden with rows of beets, chard, and various salad greens, all from seed. Next, I sowed annual corn poppies—a pastel strain called Angel Wing—between each row of greens. Everything flourished. The healthy, turgid vegetables looked wonderfully appetizing all melded together; the pale, thin poppies floated over them like crêpe paper moons. By mid-July I had enough salad to feed an army and beets coming out of my ears. I thought it was the prettiest thing I'd ever seen.

But here's what happened next. I had initially planned to pull up the spring planting in midsummer and plant similar vegetables for a fall crop. I knew this type of succession planting was done in serious vegetable gardens; I thought I simply had to have this experience to be a serious gardener. But as the time approached to clear away the first crop, I felt less and less sure about my clever plan; the garden was getting more and more beautiful every day. The poppies were blossoming like mad, knocking my socks off. Admittedly, some of the lettuces had bolted and gone to seed, but they still looked pretty. It was hard to think about pulling up all those living plants. And worse, the thought of seeing sheets of bare ground in high summer scared me silly. Be brave—stick to your plan, I told myself. Besides, I thought, Once the new crop was up and growing, the Inner Garden would look just swell—fresh and new—while the rest of the garden was in high summer glory.

One day I pounced on the greens and poppies like a bat out of hell, yanking to beat the band. Be strong, I said, over and over, as I cringed at the first sight of bare ground. About this time, the neighbor boy, Josh, came ambling round the corner of my house. This was eight or nine years ago, when he was still interested in the garden. He was forever making suggestions for outlandish planting ideas. And he'd make up cute stories, like the time he told me he'd seen twenty-five hummingbirds on one flower. Really, I said, That's fantastic— was anyone else around? He blushed at this.

Josh knew how obsessed I was with the garden and how hard I worked to keep it looking good. When he saw me pulling up those plants like a certified nut, his eyes bulged out of his head. What are you doing? he yelled. Are you crazy? Calm down, Josh, I said. I told you my plan. Everything's going to be fine. Really, you have to believe me, I know precisely what I'm doing. (I did not.) Josh stood there shaking his head in disbelief. You better stop while there's still time to fix this, he warned. And then: Do you have friends coming for the weekend? Yes, I do, I replied, knowing exactly where this was going. Oh boy, you're in trouble, he said. He wandered off muttering to himself. I felt sick to my stomach.

I had known from the start I was making a mistake, but my hands kept yanking. Why, oh why, didn't I at least pause long enough to gather my dim wits? I could have stopped— something was telling me to. I still can't believe I destroyed that gorgeous planting at the height of its power. The sad punch line is that the fall crop turned out to be a spectacular flop. August was hot and dry and seed germination was pathetic—most greens want cool temperatures in which to germinate and flourish. The few seedlings that survived looked hurt and lonely, gasping for air. Meanwhile, the rest of the garden raged on beautifully. What happened to our lovely carpet? it seemed to be saying. I had to live with the disaster the rest of the season—more than two months. It was a hard lesson to swallow, one that slapped me in the face and called me a fool. But I learned. Boy, oh boy, did I learn.

A positive note: the final harvest of beets was out of this world—striped Chiogga, white Albina Verduna, and small, sweet golden beets. I'll never forget that armload of fabulous vegetables. I placed them carefully on the chair in the garden and snapped a picture. Fortunately, I had something delicious to serve my friends on the weekend.

Most years I plant tapestry beds in the Inner Garden. I don't know a thing about textiles, much less about carpet making, and I've never been a painter. And yet I'm sure I approach my work in much the same way as a weaver or an artist. Surely the weaver must have a good sense of what her threads will do together—how they will affect each other and work in concert—before she sits down at the loom. And surely the painter must have a clear sense of the nature of his paints before he brushes them onto the canvas. Likewise, the gardener must know his plants—their colors, textures, and habits—in order to combine them well in a garden. "Habit" refers to a plant's behavior: how it presents itself to the world. Does it shoot straight up, form a tight clump, or sprawl in every direction? Learning the habits and textures of plants is paramount to good garden design, particularly when composing a border, a tapestry, or even a windowbox. When I think about the beds of the Inner

Garden from year to year, and how best to plant them, I think more about what I want the plants to do, and do *together*, than about color, fragrance, or edibility. From a design standpoint, the latter three qualities are purely subjective and have far less to do with art than with the personality and taste of a particular gardener.

This year I wanted plenty of edibles in the Inner Garden. My niece Allison, who is a gifted horticulturist and an excellent worker, was here with me for several weeks this spring, and we were too busy with my clients' gardens to get much planting done in the Inner Garden until early June. Not to worry. June in my part of the world tends to be cool, and thus gentle and forgiving to busy gardeners. Still, to get a jump on things, we planted the Inner Garden mainly with transplants and filled in after with some seeds.

On the morning we set to work, I placed all the plants first, before doing any planting. Each bed measures 4 feet by 8 feet. In each one I placed a purple cabbage, an eggplant, three kales, three romaine lettuces, and six each of the following flowers: Gem marigolds (some orange, some yellow), which have tiny blooms and ferny, scented leaves; plain, everyday marigolds (short ones with single flowers of orange and yellow); Profusion zinnias (some orange, some white); Strawberry Fields gomphrena, a red clover-like flower; and hot-pink Perfecta verbena. At the center of each bed I placed a cluster of three tallish White Nymph salvias to maybe, just maybe, cool things down a bit. I arranged the plants informally, splashing and painting the beds, keeping in mind all the while the nature of each plant and what I could expect from it. I knew the cabbages would require the most space, and the gomphrenas and verbenas the least; the other plants fell somewhere in between. I fiddled about and paced around, fine-tuning the arrangement, trying to see the finished picture in my mind's eye.

Allison and I each took two beds. For every plant we dug a generous hole and added a heaping scoop of homemade compost. Pot-bound plants had their roots gingerly disentangled before planting. All plants were firmed in to eliminate air pockets around the roots. Next, we sowed seeds of fast-growing salad greens—rustic arugula, Black-Seeded Simpson lettuce, and spicy hot Purple Osaka mustard—to thread among the plants and weave the tapestries together. Most greens have small seeds, so to ensure good distribution, we divided the three packets evenly into two bowls of compost, mixed thoroughly, and sprinkled the mixture all over the beds with spoons. Using claw cultivators, we scratched up the soil to lightly cover the seeds, then pressed it all down. Lastly, the beds were thoroughly watered in with diluted fish emulsion. In mid-June, before she went home to South Carolina, Allison thinned the salad, leaving the best and strongest seedlings to grow up among the other plants. Later, I mulched the beds with an inch-thick layer of compost.

As I write, on a very mild day in early July, the Inner Garden is robust and healthy, glistening and lush. The cabbages are 2 feet wide with dramatic, veined leaves; the eggplants have promising lavender blooms; the heads of romaine are dense and crisp; and the kale has large, frilled leaves of deep blue-green. The annual flowers are just coming on, but the ground is covered, so I'm happy as sin.

Allison's seedlings are flecked all through the beds, looking as if they simply put themselves there. Bingo! The four box shrubs and the circle of blue fescue anchor the beds, bringing order and discipline to the garden. The tire planter is bursting with red chard and looks, well, full of itself. At the moment, the Inner Garden is performing one of its most important jobs exceedingly well: serving as a lovely, rich carpet stretched before the Rear Border.

The Rear Border is planted in mixed-border fashion and forms a focal point through the main axis. The color scheme here, unlike that of the other beds, is somewhat soft and cool. Foliage drives the border early on, but in mid-July flowers kick in to double the fun. Composed of woody shrubs and late-season perennials, it remains much the same from year to year. Like all borders, it requires some fine-tuning each spring, but it's a relief to have one bed in the Main Garden that's low maintenance. The border measures just 22 feet by 4 feet, but it's packed with bodacious plants.

The standard (tree form) Pee Gee hydrangea I planted the first year has a thick stem and large head. I prune it hard each spring to keep it in bounds; it flowers on summer growth, so the resultant new stems are soon loaded with flower buds. Other plants that form the border's framework are a gigantic zebra grass (*Miscanthus sinensis* 'Strictus'); a purple-leafed sand cherry (*Prunus x cistena*); and an enormous shrub rose (*Rosa* 'Carmenetta'). (This vigorous rose has blue foliage and single pink flowers. It's okay, not great—lackluster by mid-summer. Stick to *Rosa glauca,* which is what I thought I was buying nine years ago. It turns out 'Carmenetta' is a cross between *R. glauca* and *R. rugosa,* but it lacks the good attributes of either of its parents.) Beneath and around these large plants is a middle layer of shrubs and perennials: red barberry (*Berberis* 'Ruby Glow'); joe-pye weed (*Eupatorium* 'Gateway'); snakeroot (*Cimicifuga* 'The Pearl'); and white mugwort (*Artemisia lactiflora*). The bottom layer includes lady's mantle (*Alchemilla mollis*), *Aster* 'Coombe Fishacre,' *Iris siberica,* and *Sedum* 'Autumn Joy.'

Every spring I say I'm going to lose that mediocre shrub rose. Every spring I say I'm going to divide the zebra grass, because it crowds other plants. Every spring I say I'm going to replace the purple sand cherry, because it's too dark and brooding. Every spring I do none of the above. But every summer I enjoy the Rear Border immensely, as one does a treasured friendship. After all, we have a history together: I cut my border-making teeth on it. I remember reading in Rosemary Verey's *Classic Garden Design* that a kitchen garden ought to include a "comely border." I dearly love my comely border, warts and all, especially in August. The tree hydrangea, heavy with creamy trusses, sprawls everywhere. The zebra grass rustles in the wind and sparkles in the sun. And the sedums turn into great pink buttons, strung across the front.

The Entrance consists of a double gate and two beds on either side. Just where the gates swings open, the cat-lady urns are placed like a pair of sentinels, announcing the garden ("meow, meow"). The entrance measures 7 feet by 4 feet. In the early years, this small rectangle was covered with flat stones, laid in a crazy-paving pattern. This didn't work very well; the stones tended to heave during the winter and got in the way when I opened the gates. I got rid of the stone, replaced it with grass, and set three stepping stones in it. This looked nice, and brought a touch of the grassy-green yard into the garden. But I got fed up with mowing and clipping it. I'll never forget one warm Saturday when I had a bunch of friends over for lunch. There I was on my hands and knees, clipping that silly grass, while my friends chatted merrily on the porch. I thought, Bless Pat, child, you're one sick puppy. Let this garden go for a minute! (Not a chance.)

Several years ago I ripped out the grass in the Entrance and replaced it with fine, cream-colored gravel, which I bought in bags from a garden center. After putting down the gravel, I reset the stepping stones. The gravel looks good, nice and clean, and is virtually maintenance-free. But now I wish I had used native pea gravel from one of the many quarries in my area. It would have been grayish in color, much more subtle, and in keeping with the cobble-stones and other local materials I use in my gardens.

The two beds either side of the gate are small and oddly shaped. Frankly, they've always been catchalls. I've felt from the beginning they should reflect the style and planting of the Rear Border, but I've never settled on the right perenni-als and shrubs. Actually, what I long for are two Korean tree lilacs (*Syringa*), but they're awfully expensive. I first saw this plant grown as a standard (by nature it's a shrub) in a gar-den in Connecticut. Three years ago, I planted a pair of them in a client's garden, and they're superb. (He loves the plants, but loves even better to tell me they've grown too big for their allotted space. They have not, I insist. But if you wish to part with them, simply pick up the phone.) Unlike the common lilac, this type has small, attractive leaves that don't get dingy with mildew in summer. It flowers in June in the Catskills, with scented lavender-pink blooms. As soon as the blossoms fade, I shear the plants heavily into tight, green globes. I reckon a pair of tree lilacs would be stunning, perched at the front of my garden, ruling the roost in June. And the possibilities for underplanting would be endless, given all that open ground underneath.

The best plantings ever in the Entrance beds were big fat stands of Mexican sunflowers (*Tithonia rotundifolia*), which some people call torch flowers. For anyone who likes orange in the garden, and I adore it, it's hard to beat this robust, bushy annual. Tithonia is related to zinnia and has a perfect, childish flower: large, plain petals with a circle in the middle. It's easy as pie to grow, loves heat, and flowers nonstop till frost. It wants plenty of room to really flourish— crowd it too much and it'll tell on you. I always grow tithonia somewhere in the garden, but the ones that year at the Entrance left all others in a cloud of dust. I put three small plants in each bed, 2 feet apart, after digging in plenty of manure. Those suckers went nuts. By the end of the season they were 7 feet tall and I had to use a stepladder to deadhead them. On the fence nearby I grew pale blue Flying Saucer morning glories, which flew into the heads of the tithonia and rambled everywhere.

On both sides of the stick fence by the Entrance I have clematis vines. On the right is Snow Queen, which I got by mail order from Wayside Gardens. The catalog said it was a Chelsea Flower Show winner. Enticing, I thought. It's fabulous. I planted it, oh, four years ago, and it took the first two to get well established. Now it drapes the fence and flowers for several weeks from late June into July. The petals are whispery—washed-out lavender that fades to white—and the spidery stamens are tipped with plum. It glows at dusk.

On the left side is Comtesse de Bouchard, which has elegant mauve blossoms with lots of blue in them. This was one of the first plants I bought for the garden, nine years ago. The minute I saw it for sale in a nursery I grabbed it. It reminded me instantly of my friend Sonny, who had died of AIDS a few years before. I met Sonny when I lived on Nantucket Island off and on during the 1980s. He was from Cookeville, Tennessee, and he was as smart and funny as all get out. Till the day he died he sounded like he just got off the boat from Tennessee—I loved to hear that boy talk. Sonny was a gifted, stylish gardener with a handful of private clients on the island. I worked several summers part-time for him and learned a great deal about charm and intimacy in gardens. In one of his gardens, on a trellis behind some roses, he grew Comtesse de Bouchard.

In the last months of his life, I had the privilege of caring for Sonny, whose lover, Paul, had predeceased him by several months. It was a wrenching experience at times, but very rich, and one I wouldn't trade for all the money in the world. Before he died he gave me his copy of *Hortus Third*, a massive plant dictionary. In it was a card: "To Dean, 'My Eyes,' Love, Sonny." He had lost his sight a few weeks before he died and had to move about in space on my arm. When my clematis blooms extravagantly in July—and it always does—I remember my wonderful friend and love him all over again.

My garden of sticks and stones has given me more pleasure and taught me more than I ever would have imagined possible. It's been a revelation, in such a small space, to discover so much about life and what gardening means to me. I know every nook and cranny of the garden like the back of my hand, yet it keeps revealing secrets. I've come to deeply appreciate the aesthetic power of understatement and restraint. If I happen to overembellish, or get too cutesy, the garden rebels. Above all, I've found that a garden of good structure, however small, can offer years of pleasure in refining its style.

One day a few years ago, while I was working in the garden, it suddenly occurred to me—like a bell going off—that the garden seemed about the same size as my house. I stopped working and went to get a tape measure.  Turns out my house, a boxy rectangle with no rooms sticking off the sides, has exactly the same square footage as my garden. I suppose we're all a good fit.

6. branching out

THE ONLY WAY IN AND OUT of my house is through the porch door on one side. When I decided to make my first garden and build the fence, I naturally gravitated to the yard on the other side, because it was more spacious and private. (The neighbor's house is a stone's throw from my door.) A path sprang up quickly in the front yard that ran parallel to the porch and carried me out to the garden.

At first I paid little attention to the front yard. It had a natural intimacy I liked and I could see its potential as a garden, but I was too busy to give it serious thought. After all, I didn't own this place. One decent garden would be quite enough, or so I thought. In the second year I dug a long bed across the front of the house and planted it with tall summer annuals. The plants flourished and it was nice to have flowers to enjoy as I passed through the front yard, but you could hardly call it a garden.

The next year the flower bed annoyed me: it was so pathetic and incomplete. I had learned so much in the Main Garden about the importance of good design and the relationship of house to garden. I was tired of passing through a front yard with nothing in it but grass and a well-worn path. The path and flower bed begged for a garden to go with them. I would stand on the porch, gaze into the yard, and fantasize about a new garden. Or I would place a chair in the yard and sit down, look closely at everything, and think. Then I would move it, sit down, and think some more. (This is one of the best possible ways to approach design. Walking around is necessary, too, but sitting will bring you down to earth and make you focus.) What sort of garden should I make? How will it be shaped and framed? What will the plant palette be? How will I achieve the right mood and atmosphere? Some days I saw a small paradise, alive with birds and bees and flowers and trees. Other days, all I saw was grass and the promise of lots of hard work. Finally, after four years, the picture of paradise got the best of me.

I knew I wanted to capitalize on the intimacy of the front yard and make it feel like an extension of the porch, and I knew my design should incorporate the existing path to the Main Garden. Bordering the yard is a hedgerow of sumac and wild roses that screens the house nicely from the road. Rising up behind the shrubs is a lovely big sugar maple. Beyond all this is a dark green mountainside, smack in your face, and running along the base of the mountain is a busy creek that sings at night. The creek, along with a spring in the meadow and two ponds nearby, give my place a strong presence of water. When I was planning my new garden, I thought of how the sound of the creek would bring a unique atmosphere to it at night.

I decided on a hedged garden of small trees, shrubs, and perennials. The hedge would frame the house and porch, create a roomlike quality, and provide a backdrop for a new mixed border. It would take a few years to mature, but the hedge would eventually be in scale with the fence around the Main Garden. What inspired me most was a single photograph in a lavish picture book, *The Gardens of Russell Page*, by Marina Schinz and Gabrielle van Zuylen. (This is an excellent companion to Page's own autobiographical book, *The Education of a Gardener*.) For a client in Belgium, Page had created a rectangular shrub garden, enclosed by clipped yew and filled to overflowing with lush foliage

shrubs. It was hard to tell from the photograph just how the garden related to the larger landscape, but you can be certain it did. Page excelled at linking a garden to its setting. What caught my eye, and made me return to the picture over and over, was the striking juxtaposition of the solid, formal hedge with the fluid, informal shrubs. I found the combination irresistible.

One fall day in 1995, after sketching a plan on paper, I pulled on my boots and got busy. I dug a bracket-shaped bed in front of the hedgerow, parallel with and slightly wider than the house. Next, I reshaped the existing bed along the house and made it wider, to match the width of the new bed. At each end of the yard I left openings between the beds, to accommodate the path. Over the next few days I tilled the new bed, removing rocks and weeds, and added loads of horse manure to both beds when I was finished. Then I mulched everything thickly with crumbled leaves. My plàn come spring was to plant the garden's perimeter with a hedge. The overall dimensions were 22 feet by 28 feet—only slightly smaller than the Main Garden but a much simpler, and very different, layout. Content for the time being, not to mention beat, I went inside for the winter. But not before giving the garden a simple name—Front Garden—to plant a seed in my mind for something special.

At some point during the winter, I came to my senses and scrapped an outlandishly expensive plan to wrap my new garden in a hedge of yew or boxwood. Somehow, at roughly a dollar a pop for rooted cuttings, plain old privet (*Ligustrum ovalifolium*) seemed much more my speed. I found an extrahardy variety called Amur River and bought the plants in early spring from Miller Brothers, a mail-order nursery. A bundle of short sticks with stringy roots arrived one day, and I lined them up in their beds like toy soldiers. Then I cut their heads off to make them bush out. I walked round and round the garden and tried to imagine how they would look when they grew into a thick green wall.

That first year I planted five native white-flowered trees and shrubs—*Amelanchier* 'Autumn Brilliance,' *Aronia* 'Brilliantissima,' *Halesia carolina*, *Franklinia alatamaha*, and *Viburnum prunifolium*—in the mixed border. I used five things because when I plant only a few trees and shrubs in one area I like to use odd numbers, unless I want a formal effect. I wanted the border to be informal. Next, I filled in with cheap annuals—my wallet said no to perennials. In August, when the annuals hit their stride some orange zinnias got mixed up with blue salvia, and that made me happy. Mostly, though, I fretted about the tiny hedge; nobody seemed to notice it. One day I corralled my friend Cal into the new garden. Now, what exactly are you planning to do here? he asked, looking around doubtfully. What do you mean? I screeched, *planning* to do. I'm doing it—the garden is begun! Thank heavens the Main Garden was in good form.

The following spring I made a small stone terrace in the middle of the bed along the house and furnished it with a $10 bench—plain and comfortable. This provided a place from which to view the border, the hedgerow, and the mountain behind. It also made a nice place to sit on moonlit nights and listen to the creek. I splurged on a few perennials for the border and planted a dogwood tree (*Cornus florida*), a gift from friends in memory of my mother, who had died a few weeks earlier. (Ever since, in my heart, this has been her garden.) The dogwood replaced the viburnum, which had been mysteriously beheaded when it was 6 feet tall. I came home one day in March to find nothing but a foot-tall stem sticking out of the ground. I looked all over the place for the head of that plant and never did find it. I just wanted to see it.

Still short on perennials, I filled up the mixed border with loads of tall white tobacco (*Nicotiana sylvestris*) and masses of double Shirley poppies, which I grew from seed. In the bed along the house I threw in more annuals and arranged a few pots around the bench. (The stone terrace and bench had been a good idea; the terrace itself divided the bed in half, which made me look more closely at the bed and consider how best to treat it. It was clear the bed should be planted semiformally in subsequent years, to offset and complement the informality of the mixed border it faced.) The tobacco plants shot to 5 feet, but they looked stiff because I had planted them in too much of a row at the back of the border. The poppies along the front grew into great monstrous things intent on swallowing everything in sight (too heavily fed?). Worse, they were too prissy-pink and frilly for me—like pompoms some cheerleader had stuck on top of sticks. One day in August I snapped and jerked them out of the ground. I felt delivered.

In the fall I decided that, come next spring, I would dig up the grass in the Front Garden and replace it with a stone floor. I had grown tired of mowing and clipping, and the path had turned into a muddy rut. I hated dragging the mower into the garden and hated more the way it blew grass all over the plants. I loved the plants spilling out of the beds, but clipping the grass around them was ultratedious.

Before winter I mowed the grass as low as I possibly could. Next, in order to kill it, I covered it completely with black plastic and weighted it down with bricks and old planks. (I never use herbicides. Very bad stuff—they kill the soil.) In March, I shaved off the dead turf with a flat spade, then raked and leveled the soil. This was a simple task, but not easy. It took a full day of hard work. Then I got down on my hands and knees and began laying stone, a job that stretched over many days.

Luckily, a friend who had had a flagstone walk taken up offered me all the free stone I wanted. Every couple of days I'd drop by in my truck and load up a few. Before placing the stones, I covered the ground, a section at a time, with five or six layers of newspaper to prevent perennial weeds from coming up. I worked from the outer edges in, fitting the stones together like a puzzle. Not wanting to create perfect, tight seams, I didn't cut or shape the stones. (I don't know how to cut and shape stones. When one is too big, I drop it on a chunky rock, then make the best of the broken pieces. I always close my eyes when I drop the stone, because when my Uncle Tracy was a boy he was banging on a stone for fun and a chip came flying through the air and put out one of his eyes.) Once all the stones were down, I scattered weed-free topsoil across the floor, then swept it into the cracks. I watered the soil in and left it to settle for a few days. Then I swept in more topsoil, this time mixed with seeds of golden feverfew (*Tanacetum parthenium* 'Aurea'), one of my favorite self-sowing plants.

The addition of the stone floor changed the Front Garden dramatically: It gave the space a feeling of solidity and stability that was absent the first two years. It eliminated the maintenance involved in mowing and clipping grass and the constant wear and tear on heavily traveled turf. It provided an excellent surface for furniture and pots. And it made it possible to plants things right up to the stone, where they could sprawl onto the floor and soften its edges. Best of all, the stone floor completed the structure of the Front Garden—everything was now of a piece.

It's been five years since I planted the hedge and it's grown into a thick green wall 4½ feet tall, the same height as the stick fence. I shear it three times each summer to give it a sharp line. The hedged garden sits squarely at and hugs the front of my house, so its roomlike quality fully extends the intimate feeling of the screened porch. Together they form a complete indoor-outdoor space. The porch was always one of my favorite rooms of the house; now it's one of my favorite places in the world. From here I can observe the mixed border as a single, layered composition. The border, which thrills me at times and bugs me at others, forms the heart of the Front Garden and imbues it with personality and style. But whether I fret about its problems or delight in what looks good, the planting is always enhanced by the sharp line of the hedge, which lends it order and definition. Observing the border while actually in the garden is also useful, but this causes me to focus more on individual plants and particular sections of the border and less on the big picture. Both ways of seeing are equally important and lead to critical thinking and fresh ideas about plant association.

I take the word "border" quite literally. Borders should play off a hedge, wall, fence, or other background. Island beds done in the border style can be awkward, even if expertly planted and well tended. The point in planting a border is to paint a picture, and a picture needs a frame. This device, however you decide to employ it, will do more to command the average viewer's attention than the rarest plant collection in the world.

Choosing plants for a mixed border is purely personal. One is limited only by imagination and circumstances, particularly soil, light, and zonal restrictions. The plant palette of a desert gardener is vastly different from that of a Northeasterner, but their approaches to arranging plants in a border are similar. Most important, both use plants with contrasting and complementary habits. Clever plant juxtaposition lies at the heart of all good borders. Combining a dense, fleshy-leafed plant with a loose, fine-textured one creates tension that rivets the eye. Further, repeated plant forms, colors, and combinations make a border balanced, cohesive, and rhythmic. Above all, the ground should be covered when the border peaks in its season, the plants weaving and tumbling together into one strong, painterly composition.

Now in its sixth year, my mixed border in the Front Garden has come a long way. Is it a strong composition? It tries to be. It's a work in progress, an ongoing drama on which the curtain never drops. And it never will, unless I walk away or, worse, become complacent. I go through moods and cycles with the border. Early each spring, as I contemplate the coming season, I worry that it will never be as good as the year before. Once everything is planted, and before the ground is covered, I *know* it won't be as good. But so far, every July, I've changed my mind: the border is always better. Never perfect, just better. And that's all I can ask for.

Early on in the Front Garden, even with just annuals, I tended toward a cooler, softer color scheme than that of the

Main Garden. By the time I put in the stone floor, a definite palette—blue, pink, white, and purple flowers, and plants with colorful or variegated foliage—was beginning to assert itself. (Mama loved pink and I often think this inspired the color scheme.) The perennial collection, which I fine-tune each spring, has grown considerably and dominates the planting. But I always save room for summer annuals, particularly at the front, where I love to create a collar of pretty flowers to adorn and dress up the border and spill onto the floor. And at least until mid-July, I fill gaps in the middle and back of the border with tall, ready-grown annuals that I dash out and buy in a panic. My friend Toby, a smart, witty woman with a casual air and great taste in plants, runs an excellent small nursery, Zena Green, near Woodstock. I can count on her throughout summer to have just the thing I need to save a disastrous section of the border.

I try to stick with plants that have good overall form and strong foliage, plants that hold their own through the season, whether in or out of flower. I don't mind if it's something that requires deadheading—in fact, I want some plants that do—but if it's one whose blossom dries attractively and thus continues to be interesting, then all the better. Flowers that shrivel and blow away and leave a good-looking plant behind are particularly welcome. I strive to use plants that fit with the style of the border and the general mood of the garden. Above all, I want my plants to join voices and harmonize, and not attract too much attention individually. Of course, there's always a case for letting a few things show off and punch up the picture: a handful of tall plants rising at the front of the border; plants here and there with very bold, dramatic leaves; and in strategic places, plants with forceful, architectural shapes.

The white-flowered trees and shrubs I planted years ago have matured, except for the halesia and Franklinia, both of which succumbed to girdling by rabbits in winter. The remaining amelanchier, aronia, and cornus shrubs form the border's upper, woody tier and essentially dictate the rest of the planting. Over the years I've gradually lifted their crowns by pruning away lower branches, to let in light to shorter plants, and I've eliminated awkward branches to help develop each shrub's best character.

The amelanchier, also known as serviceberry, has grown into a particularly lovely plant. Its three main stems, smooth and gray, are leafless to about 6 feet, where they branch out to form a gorgeous head of graceful, sinuous limbs. In very early spring, before the leaves unfurl, the tree blossoms into a fleecy cloud of delicate white flowers. Fruiting has always been disappointing until this year, when in June the plant was loaded with clusters of pinky-red berries. I ate a few— they're quite tasty—but the birds and chipmunks got most of them. Every day for two full weeks, I watched from the porch as a fun parade of creatures flitted through and feasted on that tree—catbirds, robins, orioles, and finches. One day I saw a striking rose-breasted grosbeak. But best of all was a pair of cedar waxwings. They came often, and several times I saw them perch right next to each other and pass a berry back and forth a few times, before one of them finally swallowed it. Heaven can wait, I thought.

The border's middle tier is composed mainly of various foliage shrubs, summer-flowering perennials, and airy grasses. I adore golden-green leaves in my gardens, and from early spring right through July, Lime Mound spiraea lights up the border brilliantly in three places. Later, when its pink blossoms have faded and the foliage has turned a bit dull, the plant's recessive color is fine, even restful, since the rest of the border is rich with flower color. In one corner, at the feet of the aronia bush, I have *Catalpa bignonioides* 'Aurea.' This large-leafed plant is actually a tree, but I cut this one low to the ground every year and it sends up several vigorous branches instead of just one, forming a dazzling green-gold shrub.

I've grown very fond of dark foliage, too, which creates depth and moodiness in any color scheme. Among shrubs that I rely on for this effect are three dwarf barberrys (*Berberis* 'Crimson Pygmy'), which are dense and bushy like the spiraeas. I have another barberry, whose name I forget, with leaves that are the same warm maroon color, but whose branches are very erect and give the border a nice bit of verticality. I'm very excited about my new ninebark (*Physocarpus opulifolius* 'Diablo'). I know it will get too large for the border eventually, but until then, I can enjoy the beauty of its purple, maple-like leaves and dark exfoliating bark.

Other shrubs in the border include *Rosa glauca*, fragrant swamp azalea (*Rhododendron viscosum*) and *Abeliophyllum distichum,* which some people call white forsythia. This plant, which grows at the base of the serviceberry bush and rambles gracefully among its lower stems, is the first shrub to flower in my garden in spring, with beautifully scented tiny white bells; the handsome green leaves that follow turn yellow in autumn. The plant, a member of the olive family, is related to forsythia, but it is more refined and tasteful in every way than its loud cousin.

Chief among perennials in the border are a dark, tiny-leafed spurge (*Euphorbia dulcis* 'Chameleon'), lady's mantle (*Alchemilla mollis*), masterwort (*Astrantia major*), and *Sedum* 'Matrona.' I have several large plants of each of them and together they make up the border's main herbaceous layer. All of them are robust growers that get about 2 feet tall and wide. The spurge, which is one of the first perennials in the garden to make a show with its rich leaves, picks up and continues the dark foliage theme. The lady's mantle, with its frothy mass of tiny chartreuse flowers in June and July, enhances everything around it. The masterwort, with shapely palmate leaves, has a crown of starry green-and-white flowers throughout July that are excellent for vases. And the sedum punctuates the border with its fleshy, sculptural leaves and solid, stout habit.

None of these plants are grouped into threes or fives, which is the way I've always heard you're supposed to plant perennials. In my small border, I've found it's much better to spread them round, keeping in mind the importance of balance and repetition. This method sets a comforting rhythm for the border that allows me to try out small numbers of new plants without causing the border to become dotty and discordant.

Other perennials include *Geranium* 'Claridge Druce,' planted near the back of the border, where they form neat, 2-foot mounds of foliage dotted in June with single rosy-pink flowers. In July, just when I think they are about to be swallowed up by taller plants, they develop long, strandlike stems that travel into the hedge and spangle it with blooms. *Amsonia hubrechtii* has pale blue flowers in late spring and fine, threadlike leaves that turn yellow-orange in the fall. The amsonias provide good contrast with the sedums and other plants with coarse foliage. For height at the rear of the border, I have several clumps of *Artemisia lactiflora,* which gets over 4 feet tall, with creamy plumes in July and August. *Veronicastrum virginicum* 'Roseum' also tops 4 feet and has wonderful sprays of pinky-white flowers at the same time as the artemisia. For spiky effect, I have three large clumps of switchgrass, *Panicum virgatum* 'Heavy Metal,' and several clumps of Siberian iris. When the switchgrass flowers in August and September, the tall, misty plumes create a dreamy, diaphanous effect in the border that's delightful, especially on dewy mornings, when they glisten.

The bottom tier of plants at the front of the border consists almost entirely of annuals, except for several clumps of *Sedum* 'Vera Jameson,' which is low-growing, with wonderful smoky-blue leaves and deep pink flowers in August. Each year I experiment with my annuals. I always try new things, but it's nice occasionally to have old favorites back. What I'm mainly looking for in my selections are plants with trailing, sprawling habits that will flow onto the stone floor and also be good companions for the neighboring perennials. I use upright plants too, but they must be good at jostling for space in a burgeoning garden. I love it best when they adapt by leaping into the perennials and shrubs.

I think of the annuals as my final brush stroke in the border; I don't plant them until after I've added any new perennials and shrubs or divided and transplanted old ones. If they are tender annuals, I don't plant them until mid-May or later; a late frost is not unheard of in my Zone 5 garden. Hardy annuals, as well as tender perennials that I grow as annuals, can be planted much sooner. "Annual" is a relative term in gardening. Many tender plants, some of which can live for years in mild climates, can be treated as annuals where winters are long and cold; they are sufficiently vigorous in one growing season to form a decent-sized plant. A trendy term, "temperennials," has popped up in recent years to categorize these plants for gardeners.

Among this year's selection of annuals is *Cerinthe major* 'Purpurescens,' a plant I grew once before, but not satisfactorily. The plants had been too long in their containers when I bought them and never did adjust well to their new home in the Rear Border of the Main Garden. As I write, in mid-July, they are flourishing to beat the band in the Front Garden. Cerinthe is a bushy thing with fleshy stalks and blue-green leaves that look a bit like those of garden peas. The small, blue-purple flowers appear as sweet nodding clusters and give the plant a feminine beauty. Mixed up with them in places are the warm pink blossoms of *Salvia* 'Coral Nymph,' borne on tall thin spikes.

A new foliage annual for me this year is *Artemisia* 'Oriental Limelight,' and what a lovely thing it is. Already 2 feet tall (the tag said 16 inches), the plants are vase-shaped and have decorative cut leaves splashed with lemon and green. Another variegated plant, and one I always have in the garden, is trailing mintleaf (*Plectranthus madagascariensis*), which has bright cream-and-green foliage with a soapy-clean scent. One of the best weavers in my garden, it rambles in all directions, threading among its friends in the border, enhancing one and all with its pretty, pretty leaves. Another good weaver is *Petunia integrifolia,* one of the parent species of modern hybrids. This marvelous plant, usually seen in containers, is excellent in flower beds too, romping about and blooming nonstop with single magenta flowers. No deadheading necessary, thank you very much.

On one side of the stone floor in front of the border I have an old Adirondack chair that I painted cornflower blue several years ago. Now faded and gray in places, it still makes a strong color statement—too strong in early spring. When the chair eventually collapses (any day now) I want to replace it with a black one. It sits at an angle with its back to the border, facing the bench in the bed along the house. On the other side of the floor I have a tall copper wash pot that I bought for $40 at a salvage yard. It's a superb piece, I don't mind saying, with a streaky patina and nice handles that look a bit like door knockers. I treat the chair and the pot, and the plants and containers I arrange around them, as related still-life compositions. I consider every component very carefully. Together, they tweak and accentuate the border behind them. In the context of the Front Garden I think of them as worlds within a world.

Next to the chair I usually place one of my best pots, with something quiet and subtle planted in it. This year, I used a tallish pot and filled it with white bacopa (*Sutera cordata* 'Snowstorm'), a trailing annual with tiny scalloped leaves and starry white flowers. On the floor next to the chair, I removed a stone, dug a hole, and planted a nice fat boxwood ball, to function as living sculpture. Just behind the shrub, a self-sown purple cleome rises from a crack in the floor. Dotted around the blue chair are ferny tufts of golden feverfew.

Another cleome grows in the floor just by the wash pot, filled this year with a towering variegated rush (*Scirpus lacustris* 'Albescens'). The rush, which has thin tubular leaves 6 feet tall, is underplanted with trailing *Helichrysum* 'Limelight' and a delightful annual, new to me, called centranthera, which has a vigorous, sprawling habit and button-like blue flowers. Near the container, nestled among golden feverfew, is another box ball, this one in a terra cotta pot. Planted in the floor nearby is a single mullein (*Verbascum bombyciferum* 'Silver Lining'), which elicits comments from almost every visitor. Its tall stems, which sway gently in a breeze, are downy-white and spangled with yellow flowers. These are the only yellow flowers in the Front Garden.

Several years ago, to establish the semiformal effect I wanted in the bed along the house, I planted four upright yews (*Taxus* 'Hicksii'), two on either side of the bench and an equal distance apart. They were small when I planted them, about 2 feet tall. No problem, I thought, I can wait. Between each pair I planted an oak-leaf hydrangea (*Hydrangea quercifolia* 'Snow Queen'). This American plant, native to the Southeast, is one of the most wonderful shrubs in the world. I'll never forget seeing it in the wild, growing on the Alabama River near my sister's house in Montgomery. Its large, handsome leaves are coarse and textured and look exactly like those of some oaks. The creamy, cone-shaped flower trusses that appear in summer are sumptuously beautiful. To boot, the plant has burnished red leaves in the fall. My pair of shrubs has thrived.

As for the yews, I dug them up last year and gave them to a friend who had just bought a house. For some reason, the plants had never taken off and I had given up on my dream of someday having dramatic, evergreen pillars lined along the house. I replaced them with four hydrangea standards (*H. paniculata* 'Tardiva'). In leaf, this cultivar looks exactly like the popular PeeGee hydrangea (it's a form of the same species), which I have in the Main Garden, but its blossoms, like those of the oak-leaf hydrangea, are cone-shaped and erect. When I saw the four Tardiva plants for sale last spring, in a good nursery that specializes in woody plants, I saw at the same moment, in my mind's eye, those disappointing yews leaving my garden. Go for it, I thought. Moments later, with my real eyes, I saw $300 leave my wallet. Oh well, the rent could wait.

The six brawny hydrangeas create a lush, textural border along the house. Restful in their green-and-white simplicity, the shrubs offset nicely the complexity of the flowery mixed border opposite them. The Tardiva standards, gorgeous in blossom throughout September last year, have almost doubled in size, and their great leafy heads are heavily set with flower buds again. This year, in sunny, open spots among the shrubs and along the edge of the bed, I planted a combination of two annuals. I used the same kind of plants on both sides in order to create balance, but I varied their placement, to blur and soften the formality of the border. To echo the dark foliage theme in the mixed border, I planted my favorite coleus (*Solenostemon* 'Garnet Robe'), a trailing plant with elegant, maroon-velvet leaves edged in green. Mixed up with the coleus is *Petunia integrifolia* 'Alba,' the white form of the magenta-flowered species.

When I first step into the garden the bench is concealed by the lush growth of the hydrangeas. I like this very much—it makes it feel like a special destination. On each side of the bench I have a pot, just like the one beside the blue chair, but these are planted with *Helichrysum thianschanicum* 'Icicles,' a subtle, upright annual with very narrow, silvery leaves. "Icicles" is a perfect name: the plant is cool and still. For three years, on the wall behind the bench, I've been training two Duchess of Edinburgh clematis, a double-white form, to climb up a pair of stick trellises I made. This spring, when the vines got to the top, I strung a horizontal line of wire between them. Every few days, I direct the stems of the clematis to grow along the wire, gently weaving them together with their tendril-like leaves. The clematis, now in flower in mid-July, creates a green-and-white frame around the bench.

I think of my Front Garden as a slightly fancy place. When I consider ways in which to improve it and make it lovelier, a certain mood creeps over me. The feeling I wish to create—the feeling I hope visitors experience in the garden—is one of intimacy and calm. I strive to make it romantic and stylish, and I keep it tidy and smart at all times. I want the garden to seem like a world apart, where all is well and beautiful. The chair and bench are arranged in such a way as to encourage socializing among my frequent guests. It's my favorite place to enjoy a glass of wine at dusk, nibble a few olives, and watch the night sky appear. The garden is my special "room," where special plants are arranged and presented in a particular way. Dare I say it? I feel pretty in my Front Garden.

I'm thrilled when people respond to the atmosphere of my garden. It fills me with happiness and gives me a wonderful sense of accomplishment. Of course, it's also nice when people simply comment on or ask questions about specific things. After all, a garden is made of many parts. This is fine, this is great—I'm mad for details myself. But I've learned that what really makes a garden and lifts it up is for its disparate components to magically coalesce into a

my favorite place to enjoy a glass of wine at dusk . . .

nibble a few olives and watch the night sky appear . . .

unified whole. Such a garden has the ability to capture and stimulate the imagination of a visitor. When I see this in my garden, I feel grateful to be breathing on the planet.

Two years ago, I had a young German woman and her American girlfriend staying with me briefly. I didn't know them well, don't recall their names, and have never seen the couple again. (They were friends of friends.) I always want to call the German one Iris, because while she was here, she buried herself for hours at a stretch in a thick Iris Murdoch novel. She practically lived in the Front Garden that summer weekend, always dressed very cutely, always sitting in the blue chair, and never without her white, floppy hat to shield her fair skin from the sun. I loved watching her secretly from the porch and see her enjoying her book in the garden. She would occasionally look up from her reading and glance about, appearing so comfortable and satisfied. Every now and then she would move to the Main Garden, sit down, open her book, and plunge back in.

When they returned home to New York City, the women sent me a nice homemade card. I've misplaced it, which is why I can't recall their names, but I remember it well. On the front was a dreamy, out-of-focus snapshot they had made of the blue chair. In their message they thanked me for the weekend and expressed how much the garden had affected them. They were terribly sincere, and I was deeply touched. Moments like these cause me to forget completely the toil that goes into my work.

The Front Garden, much as I love it, has its problems. The hedge is way too twiggy and bare at the bottom, and shearing it in high summer is getting more and more tedious the thicker it gets; the plants in the mixed border make it very difficult to maneuver around. I worry that the garden has too many frothy, lacy plants and too few that are solid and coarse, causing it to look mushy in late summer. And as I've never replaced the two trees that died, the garden looks off balance to me at times. At one end of the hydrangea border there's a hideous gully, carved by rainwater crashing down like Niagara Falls, from a bent gutter I can't seem to fix. But not to worry: when I stand on my porch gazing into the Front Garden, what I see isn't the perfect paradise I used to imagine. It's even better—it's real.

The common threads

A FEW YEARS AGO I was hired as a consultant by a woman who lives in a big country house formerly owned by a very, very famous musician. Another famous musician, to whom she is married, lives there now, but he doesn't hold a candle—well, perhaps a melting nub dripping onto the pages of rock history—to the first guy, who, along with a handful of other artists, defined the mood and spirit of the 1960s. You or anyone else who doesn't live under a rock would recognize his (the first guy's) music in an instant, and that's all I'm going to say about that. The answer is blowing in the wind.

On a damp day in June with clouds in the sky I drove to the woman's house, set deep in the woods on several acres. As I turned down the drive and approached the house, I was swept away by the sight of wild yellow foxgloves everywhere.

And I do mean *everywhere.* They poured from the woods, skirted the gravel drive, and popped out of nooks and crannies in old stone walls. I was enchanted. The spiky, pale yellow blossoms were dreamy and delightful against the rich, summer green of the forest. I like this place, I thought, as I got out of my truck and looked around.

I was greeted by Rick, a landscaper who worked for the woman. He had recommended me to his client and arranged for the consultation. "She wants flower gardens, and flowers aren't my specialty," he had explained. While we waited for the woman to appear he directed my attention to specific areas I would be expected to offer advice on. The first was a small, terraced formal garden that enticed me right away; the second was a large, sloping flower border that was in desperate need of help: it was choked with weeds. Rick and I got on fine as we walked about discussing what might be done to improve things. More than once I commented enthusiastically on the abundance of foxgloves, saying things like "Aren't they just perfect and cheerful at the edge of the dark forest, blurring the line between wood and garden?"

At last she emerged. After polite introductions we seated ourselves round a table on a brick terrace by the house. She was thin and pale, with stringy brown hair and a pointy nose. She was severe-looking but not unattractive, and she wore a big green sweater pulled tightly around her, as though she were cold and uncomfortable. When I suggested we go inside, where she might be happier, she blatantly ignored me. From the moment we sat down together she appeared to be a million miles away. As I began to comment on the setting, her house, and the garden, she glanced around nervously, avoiding eye contact with me. I got the certain feeling she disliked me, and I could tell she wasn't listening to a word I was saying. Rick sat by silently, looking as if he wanted to evaporate.

I knew in the first moments that the whole affair was doomed, that I would never sow the first seed in her garden. But there seemed nothing to do but forge ahead valiantly until I could find a way to extract myself from this torturous situation. I heard myself chattering madly on about plants and gardens, trying in vain to strike a chord with her. She had virtually nothing to say—there was no conversation— and my words sat on the ground like a bucket of wet sand. I cannot express how grim it was.

Just as I was about to launch into my euphoria over the yellow foxgloves, she looked around, turned up her nose, and asked, "What are all these yellow things everywhere?" (How could she not know? There were literally thousands of them, flowering to beat the band, in full-tilt glory.) "They're foxgloves," I said. "Do you not like them?" "Well, yes and no," she whined. "I suppose, I don't know, not really, and there are just so many of them." I explained that this particular species had been introduced from Asia years ago and had naturalized in parts of the Catskills. "It's nice to have a few wild, self-sown plants creep into the garden picture. It helps greatly to link the garden with its natural setting. Perhaps, in this case, there are too many foxgloves, but to eliminate them altogether would be a mistake and a near impossible task," I said. She had no response to this. I might just as well have been talking to a wall.

Things never got better. At some point she began yammering on about wanting a "very Ralph Lauren garden," whatever that was supposed to mean. She went so far as to suggest I drop into the Ralph Lauren shop on Madison Avenue in New York to see what she was talking about. (Huh? Was she kidding? I can just see *me* "dropping in" to Ralph Lauren.) "I'm a downtown kind of guy," I responded weakly, "but maybe, we'll see." In her desperation to be understood she kept waving her arms around wildly and talking about "plants sticking up in the air." I cut her no slack whatsoever—by this time her dislike for me was not merely obvious, it was alive and kicking and walking around on the table. I was about to jump out of my skin to end the ridiculous charade, and poor Rick had begun shifting around in his chair, fidgeting like a child about to be punished.

I can't remember who among us had the merciful good sense to pull the plug and put us all out of our misery, but someone did. As we awkwardly said good-bye she and I lied that we would "get in touch." I didn't send her a bill and I've never laid eyes on that kooky woman again, but a year or so later I ran into Rick. Apparently, soon after that June day, she had approached him: "That guy—Dean—is he gay?" she had asked. Rick was taken aback: "I don't know, perhaps he is. Yes, I would say he is. Why? Does it matter?" "Oh, well, it's just that I can't work with gay people. It simply doesn't work, I can't get along with them," she answered.

So that explains the icy reception. Not to worry, it's just as well. I may not have got along with a client who didn't appreciate the charm and practicality of self-sown plants in the garden, not to mention one who would reject a design professional based upon her assumptions about his sexuality. Actually, I'm grateful that she was honest with herself and did not feign interest in my ideas. I hope, at the very least, that she has opened her eyes to the lovely population of yellow foxgloves in her garden. And better still, I hope she has discovered that droves of gay people populate the world of gardens, gracing it nicely, much like the frisky foxgloves at the edge of her dark green forest.

Self-sown, or "volunteer," plants are essential in my garden. I have a large variety of plants for a rather small garden, and I think of my volunteers as common threads, weaving the collection together. They unify the plants and, I hope, keep the whole garden from looking too busy and cluttered. In a general way, they create a subtle link between the Main and Front Gardens, while the gardens themselves—particularly their respective plant palettes—remain distinctly different in most respects.

Any plant—even a tree or shrub—that pops up from seed of its own will can be called a volunteer. Of course, any plant can be called a weed, too, when it's out of place in a garden. The majority of plants that self-sow are annuals and biennials, and most of them germinate very freely. Many of them become weedy once they've had a couple of years to get established and fling their progeny in every direction. If they aren't ruthlessly thinned each spring they will take over like drunks at a party and hog the floor. A huge, pure stand of volunteer seedlings will look wonderful early on and make a strong statement—great masses of one thing are always very effective—but in most cases, the individuals within the masses will eventually crowd each other out.

Then they all become leggy, floppy, and unsightly, like party people with hangovers.

I thin my volunteers gradually, beginning in spring as soon as they're large enough to handle—an inch or so tall with most varieties. It's overwhelming at first to see thousands of tiny seedlings and think of reducing them in any sensible way. I start by zooming in on strong-looking ones and those I deem to be in particularly good places, clearing away all others a few inches around them. As the season progresses I whittle away at the volunteers, until only the best and the brightest are left standing. Even though I like the carefree look that volunteers ultimately bring to the garden, I'm just as choosy about them as I am about the plants I put in the ground myself. As with all things in the garden, each volunteer has a role to play in the grand scheme. Certainly, not every single one is utterly precious, but their collective impact is of great importance.

Thus far, the only perennials that volunteer in my garden with any regularity are lady's mantle and *Geranium* 'Claridge Druce,' both of which I have in the Front Garden. Neither of them seeds prolifically and becomes weedy, so occasionally, when I notice a seedling I like, I allow it to take hold— on the outside of the hedge, say, or in the stone floor, or by the porch door. Here, the young perennials are unobstructed by neighboring border plants and have ample room and plenty of sunshine to help them grow into healthy plants. Since I normally see these particular perennials simply as components of the mixed border, it's good, for a change, to observe them as isolated specimens: it causes me to focus on the plants' individuality.

I encourage annual volunteers to mingle in the beds and borders, but here they must fight for room among the hefty, established perennials and woody shrubs around them. This is fine—within a border, not every volunteer has to be a brilliant, fully developed specimen. In fact, it's much more natural, more like the real world of vegetation. Nothing thrills me more than a well-tended garden with excellent structure, great style, and carefully orchestrated plantings. But real magic comes from volunteers. They are plants that like to walk right in and sit right down, and their spontaneity does much to soften the picture.

Naturalistic gardens that include a large number of exotic plants are particularly enhanced when a few native wildflowers, however ordinary, have been allowed to work themselves into the picture. And what could be lovelier, in a decorative potager or formal herb garden, than a scattering of self-sown cottage flowers, speckled randomly around the plot. Almost any garden, really, is made more lighthearted by at least a few volunteer plants.

My friend Sarah, an artist, has a fascinating and very unusual collage-like garden that features rocks and objects combined with all kinds of ornamental plants. Sarah has loved gardens all her life, but it wasn't until seven years ago, when she was in her early fifties, that she got the chance to make one of her own. Early on, she discovered the fun and usefulness of volunteers. She says it's been very exciting as an artist to experiment with these plants that simply show up, presenting her with the interesting and thoughtful job of editing them for best effect in her garden.

My own particular volunteer army is a tough, no-nonsense lot. Most of them look after themselves almost entirely once they are up and growing, except for a handful that require a bit of deadheading and grooming. Without exception, they are sun-loving plants—though some of them are quite happy in partial shade as well—that thrive in rich soil, grow fine in average soil, and require good drainage. Most receive no supplemental feeding unless they happen to be in especially prominent places, in which case I feed them occasionally, and they are happy with a layer of compost placed round them in early summer. To keep things simple, the following list goes roughly from shortest to tallest plants. Unless otherwise noted, they are all true annuals.

Nigella damascena   Love-in-a-mist is a flower I've admired for ages but didn't have in my own garden until three years ago. My friend Larry gave me a packet of Miss Jekyll seeds, a rich blue nigella, named for the influential turn-of-the-century English gardener. (It also comes in pink and white.) Nigella is a low-growing plant in the buttercup family (Ranunculaceae) that gets about 1 foot tall and wide, with a wiry, sprawling habit. Its delicate cut leaves are fresh and whispery-thin. Each starry flower, about the size of a nickel, is held in a misty green spray and is adorned with a collection of sex parts that sits high and tall like some outrageous hat. Soon after the petals drop, the plant forms decorative seedpods that look like tiny paper lanterns. Some couturier ought to design a fabulous gown based on this remarkable little flower. My plants bloom in July, mainly in the Front Garden, where they pop up from crevices in the stone floor.

Petunia axillaris The first year I had my garden, on Memorial Day weekend, I came across some straggly petunias for sale at a yard sale down the road. My friend Adele was with me and insisted we stop. "Baby, just slow down as we go by—I can tell at a glance if it's worth our time." It was worth our time: I got my treasured cat-lady urns there that day. I almost passed on the petunias, but something about the flowers looked unusual and familiar at the same time. I grabbed them at the last minute—a dollar for a dozen. When I got home I cut the plants back and potted them in two big containers, which I put in separate corners of the Main Garden. The plants soon took off, leaping onto and rambling through the stick fence with abandon. They turned out to be what I had known in the South as climbing petunias. Petunias are in the nightshade family (Solanaceae), along with unexpected things like tomatoes, potatoes, and eggplants. Climbing petunias are not true vines, but like some other petunias, they behave like vines, wandering here and there for sunlight and support. Unlike most hybrid petunias, *P. axillaris* has smallish flowers on thin, graceful pedicels. Each year, I can count on a few plants springing up in the Main Garden. They range in color from snow-white to deep, velvety purple. Every blossom emits a spicy sweet fragrance that scents the night air.

Tanacetum parthenium 'Aureum' Golden feverfew is the most common plant in my garden, which suits me fine: among my common threads it's one of the most effective. I planted six of them when the garden was brand-new, and their descendents have been with me ever since. Feverfew is in the daisy family (Compositae). *Hortus Third* says it's a perennial, but I treat it as a biennial, because it has never been satisfactory for me in a third year. It germinates like mad in early spring and is dead easy to spot: its bright, ferny leaves are electric from the moment they appear. In the first year, the plants make neat, attractive mounds 8 to 10 inches tall that light up the garden marvelously till late fall. The plants sleep for the winter. By mid-July of the following year, they are 2 feet tall and covered in perfect tiny white daisies—hundreds of daisies that don't shatter in the wind, don't look drippy in the rain, and never need deadheading. When the plants turn ratty and get on my nerves, I pull most of them up and toss them on the compost pile. I leave a few in out-of-the-way places, where each one forms millions of powder-fine seeds.

Kochia scoparia I don't know a common name for kochia, so I call it Cousin It, because it reminds me of that character from the TV show *The Addams Family*. Cousin It looked like a bushy, long-haired wig that was alive. Kochia grows about 2 feet tall, depending on the seedling (there appears to be a great deal of variation in the species) and forms a dense, bullet-shaped plant with extremely narrow leaves; the tiny, unremarkable flowers go completely unnoticed. The foliage, which sometimes turns cranberry red in the fall, gives the plant a funny, shaggy look that makes it seem more like a pet than a plant. (People always want to stroke it—me included.) Kochia, a member of the goosefoot family (Chenopodiaceae) is related to the common weed lamb's quarter and to red orach, another volunteer plant in my garden. I grew kochia the first time from transplants I bought, but they were disappointing. It wasn't until early the next spring, when I saw masses of stringy little things all over the Main Garden, that I realized the plants had flowered and set seed. The new seedlings grew into much stronger plants than their parents had ever been. Every year since then, I've encouraged a few in the Main Garden, where they make good pets in my jungle.

Perilla frutescens 'Atropurpurea' Perilla is in the mint family (Labiatae), and like all its relatives I've ever encountered, it has square stems. It's a bushy plant, 2 to 3 feet tall, with highly scented, dark purple leaves that in certain light have a gorgeous, opalescent quality; you can see blue, green, and yellow, all in the same leaf. Perilla, called shisho leaf by the Japanese, is edible. I had never cared for it raw, but last summer, my friend Roger and his boyfriend, Eduardo, served a wonderful Japanese lunch on my porch. (I love it when my houseguests cook.) They fried some perilla leaves tempura style, which turned out to be delicious, with a salty sweet flavor and pleasing texture. Another friend told me she eats it on onion sandwiches with hot mustard. I had seen perilla here and there for years but was never swept away by it until I saw it in my friend Sarah's garden, where she had little rivers of it snaking through one area, the plants rising happily from the gravel that underlies everything in her garden. I grow perilla in my Front Garden, where its purple foliage creates dark pools among all the bright flowers.

Nicotiana langsdorffii I've grown various kinds of ornamental tobacco—another member of the nightshade family—over the years. *N. alata* is lovely and has fragrant white trumpet flowers that open at dusk. *N. sylvestris* is not so lovely to me, because it looks like a string mop turned upside down—worse, it happens to get aphids something awful in my garden. The only tobacco that's become a full-time member of my garden is *N. langsdorffii*. The seeds of this species germinate in late May and early June, but I'm always amazed at how fast it grows. By mid-July it's 4 feet tall, with broad, paddle-shaped leaves at the bottom and a stout flower stalk ready to burst into flower. It soon turns into a delightful cloud of tiny green bells. Inside each beautifully shaped blossom is a bundle of inky blue anthers. *N. langsdorffii* looks good anywhere, with anything. There is a variegated-leaf form as well, which I have in the Front Garden.

Verbena bonariensis Tall verbena is a subtle beauty, one of the ten best garden plants in the world. I haven't the foggiest idea what the other nine are. This elegant plant, a member of the family Verbenaceae, has pencil-thin stems and small clusters of tiny purple flowers. It's a perennial that can be treated as an annual, flowering the first year from seed. A cinch to grow, it likes sun or light shade, rich or poor soil, and never needs staking or deadheading. Because it's so airy, Verbena fits itself into almost every situation with ease, growing among other plants and dancing about them feather-lightly, while lifting its

verbena
bonariensis
the audrey hepburn of the garden

mildly scented blooms effortlessly into the air. It's wonderfully see-through, able to grow smack in front of shorter plants without hiding or upstaging them. Every spring, when literally millions of verbena seeds pop up in my garden, I think I'll pull my hair out. In July and August, when butterflies and hummingbirds flock to it, I couldn't care less about my hair. I call this plant the Audrey Hepburn of the garden, because of its charm and grace.

Atriplex hortensis 'Rubra' I don't recall when I first heard of red orach, or mountain spinach, but I do know I ordered my seeds from a place called Seeds Blüm, in Idaho City Stage, Idaho. The first time I grew it I coddled each seedling—until death: most of them wound up in the mouths of chipmunks and their pals. Luckily, one or two survived and flowered, setting bo-coo seeds in late summer. Orach is in the goosefoot family, and like its cousin, lamb's quarters, has tasty edible leaves. In late spring and early summer, I toss them in salad or wilt them quickly with olive oil and garlic; the leaves become tough and bitter late in the season. Orach is one of the first things to come to life in my garden. And does it *ever* come to life: in April, the beds of the Main Garden are blanketed with curious, raspberry-red seedlings. But they're wonderful—almost surreal-looking against the bare earth. Chipmunks and friends still get loads of them, but there are plenty left for me. The plants grow to 4 feet plus and have an appealing weedy look; their red, triangular leaves look good with vegetables and old-fashioned annuals, particularly sunflowers.

Cleome hasslerana Cleome is in the caper family (Capparaceae), which includes the caper bush (*Capparis spinosa*), whose flower buds are pickled and eaten. Also called spider flower, it's very easy and fun to grow. It has few problems—even deer don't usually eat it. It has outer-space-looking flowers and an interesting growth habit. A healthy cleome with room to develop makes a statuesque plant—4 feet plus—with a single main stem and lots of side branches and large, deeply cut palmate leaves. (People always say the leaves look like marijuana, but on close inspection they're quite different in color and texture and spiny on the undersides.) The rounded flower heads appear in July at the tips of the stems and open fresh blooms for many weeks, the longer the stems grow. Each bloom has four spoon-shaped petals (actually bracts) and long, tentacle-like stamens and pistils. The seedpods that develop hang on the plant and look like the world's smallest string beans. I grow purple and white cleome, but it also comes in pink and rose. When the seedlings in my garden are a few inches tall, I can tell if they are going to be purple or white, even though the plants look exactly alike; the purple ones have faint color in their leaf veins. I find this fascinating, because it reminds me that flowers are nothing more than modified leaf tissue.

Impatiens glandulifera Impatiens is in the balsam family (Balsaminaceae). Most people know the ordinary bedding type, which was ubiquitous where I grew up in the South. *I. glandulifera*—quite a different-looking plant to its relative— gets very tall and has unusual hooded flowers. One common name is balsam; another is policeman's helmet—the hooded part of each blossom looks like a helmet. I first grew it from seed I ordered from Select Seed, a nursery in Union, Connecticut, that I like very much and from which I sometimes order small plants of *Petunia integrifolia* and *P.* 'Alba.' (Their live plants are always in good shape and expertly packed.) Balsam is a robust, bushy plant that can grow to 10 feet tall. I have mine in a dampish bed on the northeast side of my house, where they reach 6 or 7 feet. The plant has thick, reddish-green stalks and long, handsome leaves with prominent midribs and finely serrated margins. The flowers (mine are pink) occur in clusters from high summer until frost and have a honey-sweet smell. Bumblebees love them. The plant develops curious adventitious roots near the base that look like tiny red toes. There's a giant balsam growing by my compost pile this year, and sometimes I reach down and touch its crazy toes—they're so cute. It germinates like crazy in the spring, but the plump seedlings are easy to thin.

Helianthus annuus   I don't usually have many volunteer sunflowers, because very few seeds ever drop to the ground to germinate. I deadhead my plants routinely in summer— it keeps them looking more presentable, more lush and green, than when they are allowed to set seed. Besides, I read somewhere that if too many sunflower seeds are allowed to fall to the ground and rot, the hulls emit a toxin that inhibits other kinds of plants from growing in that area. I don't know if this is true or false, but I figure, what the heck, why take any chances? I like growing other things

Pots on the fence

among and in front of my sunflowers. Still, as the season wanes, I stop deadheading. My mood turns melancholy. Suddenly it feels like sweet, fresh May was only just here. As the flowers fade, yellow warblers and other birds go nuts for the sunflower seeds. I love watching them perch precariously on top of the heavy, drooping seed heads and lean fully forward to peck, peck, peck for a snack.

The few sunflower volunteers that come up each year are usually more robust, and get a good deal taller, than the ones I grow in peat pots and plant myself—and that's saying something. This year I got more volunteers than ever, small forests of them in the Main Garden. I thinned them to a foot apart, and by mid-June they were 2 feet tall. Yippee! I thought, fewer holes to dig. One day a groundhog got in the garden by slipping through a big space in the stick fence and had his way with those stout beauties. He ate every leaf he could reach and bit the tops off half the plants. Oh, I was devastated, just devastated. Thank heavens I had my seedlings to replace them with! I managed to outsmart the rascal by wrapping the fence in thin plastic mesh (you have to look hard to see it.) Of course, he could tunnel under the fence in seconds if he wanted, but thus far I've been spared. I couldn't care less about the mess that groundhog has made by the tool shed, digging up the ground, and he can live under my house forever, as long as he stays out of my garden.

I fretted about those sunflowers for days, afraid the surviving ones, having lost so much foliage, would be stripped of their energy. My niece was still here, and I know she must have got tired of hearing me whine. I needn't have worried.

The plants recovered beautifully and are thriving in mid-July, dressed along their thick, towering stems with fat, green leaves. Most are beginning to open flowers at the top—mahogany and brown and rich, summertime yellow. Some plants are 7 feet tall and climbing. I call that volunteer spirit.

Melvin "the cheese" Bullock: nephew and frequent houseguest

8. basic black

I'VE NEVER PUT ON a little black dress and it's too late for all that now—I'm too big. My only appearance in drag was in ninth grade, when I somehow got talked into participating in a "womanless" cheerleading squad at school. A neighbor, a girl my age, supplied the clothes and helped me put my outfit together. I enjoyed the preparations and the buildup, but I was mortified when the time actually came to walk out the door and go to school. Horrors! I had to run around in that silly getup all day, the longest day of my life. I was the only one in the costumed bunch who didn't look like a boy dressed as a girl. The other guys were all jocks of one sort or another—not one of them looked the least bit feminine. I, on the other hand, was a dead ringer for Judy Carne in *Love on a Rooftop*, down to my miniskirt, tight sweater (over a stuffed bra), and frosted shag wig. The following week, a picture ran in the local paper. There I was, pigeon-toed and knobby-kneed, looking like a shy little girl who wasn't quite sure she looked so pretty after all.

This talk of miniskirts and dressing up brings me to the subject of basic black. I don't know women's fashion well, but I have the sense that a simple black dress is considered by many females to be an essential wardrobe item. And why shouldn't it be? It must be a cinch to throw it on or shuck it off, dress it up or dress it down, and make it look just right. One night years ago, when I first moved to New York City, I was fretting to my roommate that my sad-sack wardrobe was woefully inadequate and I had nothing to wear to dinner. "Black, child, you're always safe in black," he stated with finality, as though I could produce an Armani suit out of thin air. Did I even have any black?

I spent a fortune that winter on black clothes—a total of maybe five items—but apart from a smart Katherine Hammnett cardigan, which I enjoyed wearing for years, most of it was silly and trendy and didn't suit me in the least. One particularly absurd thing was a tailored, button-front jacket with a crew neck, flared waist, and ridiculous padded shoulders. (The eighties—need I say more?) When I saw it in a chic SoHo boutique called Parachute, I thought it was the fiercest thing I'd ever laid eyes on. It's a good thing I got some wear out of it for a couple of years, because one day I looked at that jacket and suddenly knew it was hideous. Now that I live in the country, it's nice to jump into any old comfy thing and plunge into the garden.

Oh, yes, the garden. I adore the evergreen shrub, boxwood (*Buxus* spp.), or as people in the know are careful to say, "box." In many a garden it's the equivalent of basic black—the little black dress of gardening. Box is your friend. It won't let you down, it always looks good, and it rarely complains. You can dress it up or dress it down, plant it here or plant it there. It's happy with roses, lettuce, or moss and perfect in pots by your front door. If you were to hold a gun to my head, I wouldn't be able to name—and be honest in the telling—a plant I like any better. Anyway, I don't go in for this business of favorite plants, favorite flowers. It's like asking someone to name his favorite cloud. But if I had to live with just one kind of plant, I'd choose acres of box. Vegetables, by the way, don't count in this little game. After all, one must cook and eat, and live life round the table with friends.

My affection for boxwood is deep and abiding. When I take time to admire it and truly see its quiet beauty and solid character, I'm filled with gratitude at having been blessed with a love for plants. I think it was Gertrude Jekyll who wrote that a love of beauty is a gift from God. Even as a child I was aware of box. I can remember brushing my hands over it in my aunt and uncle's garden, to feel the soft texture of its fine, leathery foliage, and enjoy its curious smell. I've heard people compare this smell to cat pee. But I disagree: cat pee odor is extremely vile and disgusting. Box foliage has a pleasing, earthy scent, particularly noticeable after a rain, when it hangs sharply in the damp air.

My Aunt Kat grew boxwood all over her garden in South Carolina in short, tight hedges or among other shrubs, clipped into neat balls. She rooted the plants herself, from hardwood cuttings and grew them in old coffee cans until they were large enough to plant in the ground. In the mid-sixties, not long after my parents bought their new house in Mauldin, Kat and Roy presented them with a dozen or so young plants to put in the yard. My aunt and uncle were always generous with their bountiful garden. Mama used to talk about how Roy would sometimes drive up in summer with a box full of vegetables and simply leave them by the kitchen door, without ever ringing the bell. He was a painfully shy man, but with a heart as big as the ocean.

When Kat and Roy sold their farm over fifteen years ago and moved to a retirement home, Daddy bought Roy's last pickup truck, a '77 Chevy. Five years ago, with only 60,000 miles on it, my father gave it to me. I'm still driving it. When my brother happened to mention to Roy that I had his old

truck, he just said, "Well, that truck's never been to New York." One day, several months after I got it, I was cleaning behind and under the seat of the truck—more out of curiosity than anything—when I came across some empty seed packets for cantaloupe, beans, and squash and a faded grocery list of Kat's: sugar, flour, tea, oleo. Less than two hours later, my brother called to say Roy had passed away. You tell me there's not something going on in the cosmos.

Daddy planted the new boxwoods in a straight row along the edge of the carport, to form a hedge between it and the yard and to make it slightly more private. Box is a slow-growing shrub, so it took a few years, but eventually, the plants, with the help of Daddy's clippers, formed a nice solid hedge about 3 feet tall. In the last years before he died, my father began to lose his touch in the yard. He did what he could, and Mama helped on occasion, bagging up leaves and such, but bless their hearts, they were just getting too old for it. For some reason, after years of watching those shrubs slowly fill out and mature, Daddy decided one day they needed "some of that growth cut out of them." So against my mother's wishes, he hired somebody to prune away most of the lower branches, leaving a big row of old, gray sticks with some green fluff at the top. When I saw those slaughtered shrubs, I asked my mother why in the world he had done such a thing. "Honey, I tried my best to get him to leave those boxwoods alone, but you know how your daddy is."

Long before the boxwood debacle, I had revamped the plantings at the front of my parents' house. This was one of my first design efforts after completing horticulture school and working in England. The Japanese hollies that had been there for years had become huge, blocking some of the windows, so Daddy had had them removed. There was a wide porch across the house, shaded by a broad southern red oak and furnished with two rocking chairs and a swing. "Just put me some things in with different kinds of leaves," my father had requested. On either side of the porch, I dug serpentine beds and filled them with various deciduous and evergreen shrubs: oak-leaf hydrangeas, viburnums, iteas, arborvitaes, and aucubas with gold-speckled foliage. In front of the shrubs I planted two kinds of hosta, and in front of those I planted a border of variegated liriope—a short, grassy ornamental common in the South. It was autumn, so

I added some grape hyacinth bulbs (*Muscari armeniacum*) to sprout among the shrubs and perennials in spring. It wasn't a sophisticated planting, but it wasn't too bad, either. And after all, I had to start somewhere as a designer. Besides, my parents were tickled.

As is always the case when I'm gardening, and particularly when I'm breaking new ground, I wandered around from time to time during my work, to stretch and take a break and consider possibilities for new gardens in other parts of the yard. I found myself looking at the boxwood hedge over and over. It faced southeast, and before it lay a piece of flat, sunny ground. What a nice backdrop it would make for a flower border, I thought.

I never got around to more garden making for my parents, but the plants at the front of the house thrived. The hostas flowered, sending up stalks of lavender, lily-type blooms that attracted the attention of my mother's friends. More than once she asked me their names: "Honey, what are those short, bunchy things with the tall flowers—everybody's always asking me about them?" (As *if* they were the least bit unusual.) "Those are hostas," I'd remind her. "Tell the ladies to plant them in shade and they'll come back each year." "Hostas, hostas—that's right," she'd say in frustration. "I *declare*, I always want to say 'pastas.'" "Pasta" wasn't an everyday word in my mother's vocabulary—it was spaghetti or macaroni to her.

In one of their several books, *A Year at North Hill*, Joe Eck and Wayne Winterrowd, who have gardened in southern Vermont (Zone 4) for over twenty-five years, speak of boxwood's "soothing rhythm of dark green." How beautifully put. I had the pleasure several years ago of meeting Joe and Wayne in their extraordinary garden, one of the best I've ever seen and, because of its extensive plant collection and brilliant design, one of the most important in North America. I was there to interview them for a story I was writing for *Gardens Illustrated.*

Upon my arrival, on a cold and beautiful November day, the men greeted me in the front garden before I had time to knock on the door. They were making their way down the stone steps that lead from the charming wood-shingled house into their large, paradisiacal garden. All around me was this renowned plant collection I had wanted to see for years, yet what first caught my eye was the simple, tasteful planting that adorned the front of the men's house. On each side of the door were large bushes of native winterberry holly (*Ilex verticillata*), covered with gorgeous scarlet fruit and swaying in the chilly breeze. Stretched before the hollies, like fat green ribbons binding them to the house, were neat rows of clipped box. Later, over a delightful lunch of chowder, crusty bread, and greens from the garden, I watched through the window by the table as birds hopped about in the hollies, enjoying their own meal of plump red berries.

Joe and Wayne grow various kinds of boxwood—there are about thirty species and many cultivars in the world—throughout their 7-acre garden. Some of them are too tender to withstand the harsh Vermont winters without protection, so the men have made boxes for their box shrubs—covers that fit over the plants and shield their evergreen foliage from the cold, desiccating winds. But they also grow, and highly recommend, the Sheridan hybrids, a selection of extrahardy cultivars introduced by Sheridan Nursery Company in Ontario, Canada. This excellent group of shrubs is now widely available, at least in the northeastern part of the country, and includes several cultivars, each with a different form and habit. Joe and Wayne were the first to mention these hybrids to me. I already had box growing in the Main Garden, and I knew it to be the cultivar Green Gem, but it wasn't until I got home, and consulted Michael Dirr's *Manual of Woody Landscape Plants* that I realized mine was indeed in the Sheridan group. Lovely—no wonder they had always been so satisfyingly hardy.

Green Gem has been in my garden for seven years. The plants, in gallon containers when I bought them, were no bigger than a cantaloupe. Now they're 2 feet wide at the bottom and 16 inches tall. Each one is a perfect, dense mound, completely foliated to the ground. I shear them closely once a year in early spring as soon as I see the lateral leaf buds beginning to open. I use plain grass clippers, which might horrify some people, but I find it to be the perfect tool for the job. I like to shape my box shrubs as symmetrically as possible; the clippers, being a small hand tool, allow me plenty of control in the process. I use this particular set of clippers for nothing else. When the blades finally become dull, I buy a new set and use the old ones for clipping grass, a job I don't take nearly as seriously. To speed up the work, I've tried using hedge clippers and an electric trimmer, but neither gives me the clean finish and perfect line I seek. Besides, my method allows me to spend quality time with each treasured box shrub.

The plants take a few weeks to really flush out with new growth, but by early summer they're vibrant with fresh, emerald foliage and look ever so smart and classy with the flowery things around them. The one major cut in spring is sufficient to maintain their form and density. As the season wears on, I have to nip off a few odd, feathery shoots. But I don't mind that they lose a bit of their severity and develop a soft, rippled look. The box shrubs, whose leaves become dark and burnished in winter, give me great pleasure when so  much—almost all—of the garden is bare. On many a winter day I've squatted beside one of my plants, stroked it over and over, and marveled at its classic beauty.

In a client's garden nearby, I planted boxwoods to mark the corners of two identical square beds. Here I used another of the Sheridan hybrids, *Buxus* 'Green Velvet,' which has a slightly more vigorous growth rate and more rounded shape than *B.* 'Green Gem.' These I have to shear twice each season, in early spring and in midsummer. As the plants are near the street in front of a small retail shop, they take some abuse. Generally, people are very respectful of the garden, but one winter day I saw a child, a toddler, standing on a dingy mound of snow in one of the beds, kicking one of the box shrubs repeatedly. Maddening though this was, it was understandable—children can be monstrous.

But what floored me was that a man who I took to be the boy's father stood by watching the child, apparently oblivious. I took a deep breath, informed the man of my personal interest in the shrubs, and kindly asked him to "deal with the boy." I'm glad I wasn't shrill (I have been in similar instances), because when I spoke, the man seemed suddenly embarrassed by his child's misbehavior and stopped him instantly.

In my friend Kate's vegetable garden, I planted another Sheridan cultivar called Green Mountain, which is more upright than the previous two and has a domelike shape. The plants have been in the ground four years now and are already fat and lovely. They line the main path of the garden and accent the beds in which they are placed. One spring, when the boxwoods were still quite young, I underplanted them with red and green leaf lettuce. Later, when the lettuce had gone by, I replaced it with *Petunia* 'Purple Wave' and *Zinnia linearis*, a sprawling annual with yellow-gold daisies. The two flowers got mixed up together and looked bright and pretty, spilling from beneath the box and onto the garden path. Now the shrubs are too broad and close to the ground to underplant with anything, let alone sun-loving annuals. And box is a surface-rooting plant, so it's not a good idea to dig too near it.

In his book *Manual of Woody Landscape Plants*, Michael Dirr lists a frightful number of possible problems with box—everything from canker and blight to nematodes and mites. I remember my father having a problem with boxwood leaf miner, but thus far my plants have been pest-free. I think they like my slightly acid, well-drained, loamy soil. I never use fertilizer on them, but each spring I place a layer of manure or compost around each shrub. In very snowy winters, it amazes me that they can be completely buried for weeks, yet appear none the worse for it come spring. The snow immediately surrounding the shrubs disappears more quickly than it does a few inches away. This comforts me, because it tells me the plants have warmth in them.

Boxwood may not be everyone's cup of tea or look appropriate in certain landscapes. I can't, for example, quite see it in a desert garden. But I can think of few other places where it wouldn't look right at home, given that it was happy with its conditions and the nature of the climate. As for personal preference, I know of at least one person, now deceased, who abhorred boxwood. My friend Cal loves to tell about how his grandmother, Nanny Rush, a cantankerous bird who spent her life in Virginia, once had masses of old box dug up and hauled away when she moved into a house where it was growing in the yard. The woman had a mortal fear of snakes and claimed they nested in old boxwood. Whether she was right or wrong, I have no idea. But one thing's for sure: Nanny Rush had zero appreciation for the little black dress of gardening.

pots and pans

GARDENS ILLUSTRATED RAN A PIECE years ago about a French woman and her Provençal garden. The photographs captured a shimmering world of gray-green shrubs, beautifully shaped into mounds and orbs, and low, undulating hedges. There was pale, weathered stone all about and the brilliant blue sky of the world. Leafy evergreen loquats, blossoming quince trees, and columns of Italian cypress grew in the garden. It wasn't a flowery place—a bit of yarrow here, some hollyhocks and valerian there. It was a minimal, sculptural garden, a soft and moody space filled with light and texture. There were clean gravel paths and lovely places to sit, and I wanted instantly to be in the garden and meet this fascinating woman who seemed so absorbed in her art. A striking photograph showed her, dressed in pastel-colored

163

clothes, holding a pair of green secateurs. Her skin was leathery and brown, and her hair, pulled tight into a neat bun, was white as ice. In the article, titled "Rhapsody in Green," the woman said it all, succinctly: "Textures are my story." She also said plants in pots held no interest for her because she did not plan on ending her days as a "slave to the watering can."

Those words have stayed with me. They make good sense, but I hope the time never comes when I don't have at least a few pots to water in my garden. Too many containers clutter the garden and spoil an otherwise serene, cohesive picture. But a carefully chosen, well-placed selection of pots, like special objects in a room, give the garden an atmosphere of domesticity unmatched by anything else. And I enjoy watering plants in containers. It's a good time to pause from other work, enjoy a meditative moment, look around and really see things—see birds and clouds and the world as it is. On the other hand, a great slew of potted plants will keep you running around like a chicken with its head cut off, trying to keep them alive.

Even gardens made up entirely of containerized plants— those on rooftops and decks, for example—are more practical and aesthetically pleasing when a few large containers are used, instead of a lot of small ones. Last year, when I took over the design and planting of a New York City roof garden, the client requested that I keep the plantings simple and the space uncluttered. She felt that the large, built-in containers were quite adequate and didn't want more than a handful of pots, for herbs, to be added to the garden. In theory, I agreed, but in her basement were several fine Italian terra-cotta pots that I could not get off my mind. They were plain, sandy-colored, and very shapely, and I was dying to use them. In midsummer, while she was off on one of her exotic trips, I broke down and planted them with late-season flowers and put them in strategic places in the garden. When my client returned, she didn't like the new look, but she was very sweet about the whole matter. I appreciated her honesty and removed the pots. Afterward, I could see that she had been right. Restraint is difficult in gardens, but so important. The happy ending is that she gave me three of the pots to take home.

I'm very particular about the look of my containers and the plants I put in them. I care little for highly decorative pots, which often compete with the plants growing in them. Besides, they don't suit my modest country garden at all. Simple pots with clean lines are more to my liking (no precious cherubs or apple swags for me), and I'm attracted to unusual shapes—oval pots, shallow pans, and bowl-like containers. Unless it's a very large container, I rarely use more than one or two kinds of plants. This business of cramming ten different things together doesn't appeal to me; it reminds me of those hippie salads with everything in them except the kitchen sink.

I want my containers to complement the garden and accentuate its style. A good composition, even a simple one, requires thought and sensitivity. In every case, I aim for a harmonious combination of plant and pot, one enhancing the other. In choosing a plant for a particular container, I consider all its characteristics, not just the leaves and flowers. In fact, I think mostly about the plant's habit and cultural requirements. If the container is broad and squat, I usually plant it with something low, tight, and sculptural; succulents are excellent for this purpose. If it's shallow, I always use a drought-tolerant plant. When the roots fill up the pot, I won't have to worry if I occasionally forget to water it.

One of the first things I do each spring, after the garden is tidied, is to place my empty containers, particularly the large ones and those I use in key places. I move them around to different positions, over and over, to consider possibilities. This gets my juices flowing; I get ideas about what kinds of plants to put in them based upon where I might use the pots. Even though the beds and borders are largely bare at this time, and the weather is often too cold or wet for serious work, it's great fun, after the long winter, to spruce up and begin styling the garden in anticipation of the coming season. I believe in making the most of the garden at all times, and this creative exercise makes the garden feel like it's up and running long before it really is. If the weather is the least bit decent, I'm out till dark most nights, hungry, chilly, and elated and dreaming the summer picture.

Like many gardeners, I have stacks of ordinary clay pots that I use in various utilitarian ways. But most of the containers I feature in the garden in prominent places have a story. Occasionally, something special catches my eye, but because I prefer to keep my collection to a minimum, I don't usually acquire more than a couple of new pots per year.

I have a few old clay pots that belonged to my Aunt Kat, and I treasure them. They are not fancy, but each of them is different in shape, size, and color and all have lovely patinas. The quality of the clay is better, more durable, and thicker than what you normally find these days among everyday terra-cotta. One is a short, fat, bulb-forcing pot that I planted last year with hens and chicks (*Sempervivum* 'Wolcott's Variety'). At the end of summer I brought it into the house, where it was lovely for months in a sunny window, the light playing on its thick, pointy leaves. The plant came through the winter just fine and is back in the garden this year, flowing nicely over the edge of the pot and with a coppery pink tinge in the leaves. I water this plant maybe twice a month, by sitting the pot in a bowl of water. The other day, it drank two bowlsful in quick succession.

Another of Kat's pots, a tall 10-inch one with a deep reddish brown color, has a chipped rim that looks just right. This year it's planted with a strawflower (*Helichrysum bracteatum* 'Golden Beauty'), whose cheerful, yellow blossoms look very nice indeed with the richly colored pot.

My friend Howard gave me four French melon pots as a host gift years ago, when he was visiting for the weekend. I don't know why they're called melon pots, but I have a theory. The pots are small and square with no bottoms; I figure they were made to fit over melon seedlings in the field, so that the stems, while young and tender, could be draped over the sides of the pots, thus keeping them from touching the damp ground and possibly rotting. Whatever the case, the pots are absolutely superb. They had been fitted with metal plates made with holes in them, so they could hold soil and still drain. Howard got them at Treillage, a very upscale antiques and garden shop on Manhattan's Upper East Side, of which he is the manager. They cost $30 each, so I couldn't have touched them with a 10-foot pole—certainly not four of them.

The melon pots have a marvelous texture and their earthy pink color is one you see in sunsets. I planted two of them this year with *Sedum pachyclados,* a tiny stonecrop with fine, pale green leaves. The plant makes a small, neat mound you can't resist touching. I have one of them on the arm of the blue chair in the Front Garden, where the pink pot looks fabulous and I can sit, caress the sedum, and admire its special beauty. I have the other one on top of a post by the gate to the Main Garden, another convenient place to commune with the plant.

Two years ago, while attending the annual North Hill Symposium in Vermont, an exciting daylong event organized and hosted by Joe Eck and Wayne Winterrowd, I bought a small Guy Wolff pot. Wolff is an American potter based in Connecticut who produces excellent hand-thrown pots based on European traditions. The pieces he makes himself are highly sought after and expensive. A very good quality, less exclusive line is available through P. Wakefield and Company, in Cambridge, Wisconsin. Joe and Wayne had a pot specially commissioned for the 2000 symposium; at $35, I simply had to have one. It's elegant and simple, 7 inches tall by 8 inches wide, and it has a curious, dimpled rim—its only decorative touch. I adore every inch of it.

This is not the kind of pot I want to hide with a plant. Last year I planted it with *Pelargonium* 'Vancouver Centennial,' a snazzy annual with leaves of orange and olive green. The plant grew into a nice ruffled mound with scarlet blooms in harmony with the rich color of the clay pot. This year, I planted it with one Swan River daisy (*Brachycome* 'City Lights'), whose lacy green leaves and tiny pale flowers look as good with the pot as the geranium did. Brachycome is normally seen in combination with other plants; my use of it makes it easy to appreciate its delicate, feminine beauty up close. I don't know whether my pot was fashioned by Wolff himself, but I'd like to think so. I have it displayed in the garden on a table between two chairs, where it can be properly admired by my guests.

Like the Wolff pot, my kooky cat-lady urns at the front of the Main Garden are ornaments in and of themselves. The last thing I wish to do is hide them with something blowsy and bright, which would fight with the urns and be horrid and vulgar. I planted the urns this year with a coarse succulent that has flat, blue-gray leaves: *Kalanchoe pumila* 'Dwarf Blue.' One of the reasons I like succulents in containers is because they have such interesting form and texture. When they are well presented in pots, it heightens this characteristic and draws attention to the plants as living sculpture.

The urns, made of rough concrete, are 18 inches tall by 11 inches wide, and look almost neoclassical. Were it not for the porcelain doll–like faces embedded in their sides, they would appear quite solemn. But I love how this bit of whimsy enlivens and sets them apart—how playful. The urns are one off, totally original, and most people smile when they see them. My friends, Steve Gross and Sue Daley, fine photographers who have a house north of here, remarked on the cat-lady urns immediately when they first saw them. When I told them I had got them at a yard sale just two miles down the road, they told me about an out-

one of the
Cat Lady urns

to me they
are peerless

sider artist, now deceased, who had lived in the mountains very nearby, where he made all sorts of concrete objects. I told *them* about a house up the road, where four unusual concrete pots, adorned with colored tiles, are perched on a stone wall that separates the house from the road. I do believe the pots, and my treasured cat-lady urns, are Catskill-made. Skillfully made, I don't mind saying, right here in this green valley.

For Christmas last year, my niece Allison gave me a wonderfully crude concrete pot that has bits of wood speckled through it, which gives it a very nice look. I was so delighted when I opened it. This past spring, I was excited about my new container, so it was the first thing I took out of the shed and placed in the garden. It's short and squat, not unlike Kat's bulb pot, but it has a very wide rim. I planted it with the same kind of sempervivum—*S.* 'Wolcott's Variety.' The plant quickly filled the pot and looks perfect in it; the succulent's coarse, fleshy leaves are in accord with the rough concrete.

I grow herbs in pots. They get too swallowed up if I put them in my densely planted beds. Most herbs, particularly the shrubby ones, like rosemary and lavender, want room to breathe, or else they blacken and rot. At least they do in my garden. I'm sure the natural humidity in this part of the country doesn't help. Herbs are nice in pots. Their understated beauty enhances almost any container. I have a big terra-cotta bowl that I planted last year with a fragrant tapestry of creeping thymes—lemon, silver, and woolly. I've used the same container in spring for lettuce and Johnny-jump-ups. This year, I have a big pot of lemon verbena (*Aloysia triphylla*) in the Front Garden, nestled among some lady's mantle, right by the path, where I can rub the scented leaves as I walk by. Someday I want a whole garden of herbs—an intimate, textured world, heady with scent and drenched with sunshine.

One of the best container plants to appear in recent years is calibrachoa, which goes by the trade name Million Bells. It's a petunia relative, and there's no mistaking this: the plant has a trailing habit, narrow leaves, and trumpet blooms. But the leaves and blooms are much smaller than those of petunias, and calibrachoas, generally speaking, are more refined plants (*Petunia integrifolia* and *P. integrifolia* 'Alba' are notable exceptions). They have a more tidy appearance than petunias, without being the least bit stiff, and they don't require deadheading to remain vibrant and fresh with blooms. Million Bells comes in pink, white, yellow, apricot, and blue, and my favorite, Terra Cotta, whose flowers are splashed with warm sunset colors. It's sweet as all get out—I cannot get enough of it.

Calibrachoa lends itself beautifully to all kinds of pot culture. I saw it thriving in window boxes last summer at the Plaza Hotel in New York. There were two or three colors of it mixed up with bidens, a good plant with ferny leaves and yellow daisy-type blooms. Don't get me wrong, it was a lovely sight, but I couldn't help thinking how much more effective and tasteful the planting would have been had the boxes been filled with just one color of calibrachoa and no bidens. I mean, here you had this ornate, venerable building—it simply would have been better served by a simple planting. Bright color wasn't the problem—after all, it was high summer—but the jumble of color was a bit naïve in this particular situation.

You see this dotty approach to container planting wherever you go in the world. I'd be a rich man if I had a nickel for every time I've seen a whiskey barrel sparsely planted with purple and white petunias, yellow marigolds, red geraniums, and one of those things called "spikes." (What are they anyway?) None of the above plants are personal favorites, but a barrel filled to overflowing with any single one of them would be much more effective and likable than dots of all five.

I love coleus (*Solenostemon*) in pots, and there are so many good ones to choose from now. When I was growing up in the South, coleus was almost strictly a shade plant, but now there's a huge range of sun-loving ones available. It's easy to go overboard with them—their jazzy foliage is irresistible—but used sparingly, their boldness makes them good accent plants. Just today I moved a pot of Dark Heart, which has very patterned leaves of maroon and green, from the porch steps and into a new position in the Front Garden, where I needed something to punch up a mushy spot. I placed it on the stone floor, just in front of the border, nestled among some verbena and sedum spilling from the bed. Sometimes, if I have a dull spot in the mixed border itself, but it's too dense and lush to actually plant in, I simply pop the plant, pot and all, right down into the border. This works best if the pot is totally hidden by surrounding plants, so no one knows I've cheated and patched up the picture. The trick is to remember to water it.

Blue Meadow Farm in Montague Center, Massachusetts, is one of the best retail nurseries in the Northeast. I first heard about it from my old friend and horticulture teacher in North Carolina, David Carson. David retired to Massachusetts, where he had grown up, and wound up working part-time for Alice and Brian McGowan, the delightful couple who own the nursery. The McGowans stock a tantalizing range of mainly herbaceous plants. For a short while, Blue Meadow sold plants through the mail, but now they offer on-site sales only. They have an unparalleled selection of coleus: the 2001 catalog lists over seventy-five varieties. Check out some of the names—they're a hoot: Awesome Critter, Electric Kool-Aid, Inky Fingers, Jungle Love, Lucky Pucker, Radical Butter Bean, Schizophrenia. I used to think hostas and daylilies had the kookiest names in the business, but now I've changed my mind.

I've not grown any of the above coleuses, and most of them sound a bit too wacky for me. The ones I like best have subtle variegation or almost solid foliage. Penny, which has dark stems and large, sulfur-colored leaves with pink undersides, is one of the finest coleus I've seen. The Line is choice, too, with its limy leaves and purple venation. In my experience, some of the new coleus lack vigor; Black Magic has fantastic, blue-black leaves edged in green, but I've tried it twice, and both times the plants just sat there, barely growing.

Many ornamental grasses are good in containers, because unlike some other perennials, they make presentable plants in one summer season. And the winter-hardy types can come out of their pots and go into the ground in fall, thus giving you more bang for your buck. Last year, I potted several *Calamagrostis* 'Karl Foerster' plants and put them in a new garden I was making. In late summer, when I had some ghastly holes in the Front Garden, I slipped three of them into the mixed border, where they made excellent vertical accents, saved the planting, and kept me sane. *C.* 'Karl Foerster,' which forms a tight bundle of strong, pencil-thin stems about 4 feet tall and a fountain of narrow leaves at the bottom, is one of the first grasses to flower in my garden, in June. The green stems and flower plumes turn straw-colored in August and remain attractive well into winter.

I make my own potting mix for containers by combining two parts commercial growing medium with one part manure or compost. Unlike plants in the ground, whose roots can go in search of moisture and nutrients, container-ized plants rely completely on limited reserves of "soil." Artificial growing mediums like Pro-Mix are specially designed for use in containers; they are lightweight, soil-less mixes made from organic materials such as peat moss, per-lite, vermiculite, and ground bark. But they possess very lit-tle nitrogen, phosphorous, and potassium (N-P-K), the major nutrients that virtually all plants require. I supply these by incorporating a slow-release fertilizer into the mix at the time of potting, and through regular liquid feedings during the growing season. By adding compost and manure, I enrich the potting mix and give it some guts, which makes it feel more like real soil. Of course, I have to maintain a somewhat fluffy quality in the potting mix so that it drains well; when I feel it's too heavy for a particular container planting, I simply add a little perlite to the mix.

For a few months in the late eighties, while living in Atlanta, I shared a house with two friends in a rundown neighborhood on the east side of town. I had a container garden there that turned out to be a great comfort to me during a very sad time. On a deck off the kitchen, I had assembled a collection of barrels, pots, and boxes and jammed them with bright flowers. Under the house, in a dirt-floored basement, I found a comfy, low-slung metal chair, which I placed among the potted plants. I called my creation "The Garden." I worked as a waiter at the time, so this was my only hands-on gardening. The deck didn't get a speck of shade all day long, so I had to water like the dickens against the hot Georgia sun. By late summer, the garden was a mass of flowery color.

I lived with my friend Mark, who had AIDS, and our friend Ron, who had come from Nantucket Island to help me care for Mark, during what were to be the last few months of his life. In mid-September, I gave up my restaurant job—because I could, and because Mark was beginning to require full-time care. At this stage, he was so weak that he rarely got out of bed. Ron and I never left him alone in the house. One day, a good friend of Mark's, who was visiting from out of state, offered to look after our sick friend while Ron and I took breaks. I don't remember what Ron did, but I went to lunch alone, where I drank too much wine and sobbed into a napkin. Not a pretty sight, but I could not have cared less.

As I was leaving the restaurant to return home, I ran into a woman I knew casually, who could see that I was upset. She knew Mark, so I told her frankly about his grave condition. "Oh, my God," she said, a sudden look of horror on her face, "do you have it, too?" I thought, Good heavens, woman, have you no decorum? "No, my dear," I replied, "I happen to be HIV negative. And please don't take this the wrong way, but what you just asked me was beyond inappropriate. Think about it." And I left the restaurant.

When I got home and parked my truck by the deck, the first thing I noticed was that a big pot of pink zinnias, which I kept at the top of the stairs, had fallen to the ground and shattered. Had it been the wind? How strange—nothing else seemed the least bit out of place. Oh, well, I thought. I cleaned up the mess and forgot the matter. Until several hours later, when Ron and I were sitting in the living room and all of a sudden he noticed that the VCR was gone. Without moving from the sofa, we saw that a jar of coins and a $20 bill were also missing from the coffee table in front of us. In Mark's room, where he had been in bed all day, I could see that the drawer of his bedside table had been rifled through. His wallet was gone. Suddenly, the zinnia mystery was solved: the absconding thief had obviously knocked over the pot of flowers as he made his getaway down the stairs.

I soon discovered, to my dismay, that the visiting friend, ignoring my instructions, had left Mark alone in the house that afternoon. He hadn't been away long, but it was still inexcusable. He apologized profusely, but it was hard for me to get over his irresponsibility. "Look what happened in your absence," I said. I couldn't have cared less about the broken pot or the VCR, but the thought of Mark being in danger was horrifying.

It was disturbing to think someone had been casing our house, knew there was a defenseless invalid inside, then made his move the moment we let down our guard. And it was sickening to know the thief had actually gone into

Mark's room and stolen from him while he lay helpless in the bed nearby. It was chilling to realize someone could be so wretched and dissolute, so dead in his soul, as to take advantage of a dying person.

Weeks earlier, when Mark had still been up and about, he was sitting in a chair one day by the sliding glass doors, gazing into the garden, where bees and butterflies worked the blossoms. He had always been quiet and introspective, and that day, as he sat with his head against his hand, looking outside, he had a faraway look in his eyes. I was standing at the kitchen sink, washing up dishes, feeling the silence, when Mark said, "Maybe someday I'll be able to come see you and your flowers when I move on to the great beyond." I stayed busy at the sink and tried to remain composed.

Mark died in early November, just shy of his thirtieth birthday. One bright day, shortly after his funeral, I flopped down on the deck, flat on my back, to soak up the warm sunshine. The garden had not yet been frosted, and many of the annuals were still going strong. As I lay on my back looking up at the brilliant blue sky, I remembered my friend's sweet words and cried till my heart felt better.

work detail

I CAN'T DRAW. When I try to draw a cow it ends up looking like a piece of fungus. When I was little, my mother used to let me dig through her pocketbook in church to find a pencil and a piece of paper so that I could doodle while the preacher droned. I drew elaborate curlicues and interlocking circles that looked okay, but they seemed so pointless. I usually gave up and went back to spinning Mama's wedding rings around on her finger. I was totally amazed when somebody once showed me how to draw a simple box. I still draw boxes on occasion, just to remind myself that I can't draw.

I have a lot of respect for professional draftsmen and good landscape architects, and I highly recommend their services for large, complex projects. But almost anyone can learn to design a simple garden on paper, breathe life into it outside, and develop his or her own work methods for planting and tending it. My approach to the practical side of gardening is far from perfect, but I get results, so I thought I would share it with you.

Designing

I've learned most of what I know about garden design on the ground and in the dirt. I don't use a computer for designing gardens, so if you're that advanced, you might want to skip this section. I also visit other gardens as much as possible, and I read, read, read. When designing a new garden, the first thing I consider is the house: I want the new garden to relate to it, be in scale with it, and respect its architectural style. Next, using ropes, sticks, or rubber hoses, I create imaginary beds and paths on the ground, to get ideas about how to shape the garden. Once I've settled on something, I use a simple architect's scale (it's one of those doodads that looks like a three-sided ruler—very inexpensive) and a blank sheet of paper (graph paper is probably better) to create a skeleton of the garden in miniature. I rarely draw in plants, because when I do, I make a mess of my nice clean design. I simply do the drawing so that I can hold the garden in my hand, so to speak, take it out to dinner with me, and think about how to plant it—and so that when the time comes to lay out the garden, I'll know exactly how to shape the beds and paths and what their sizes should be. Finally, using a half-moon edger—a long-handled tool with a thin half-circle of steel on one end—I cut the design of the garden into the ground. Then I start digging it up.

Tooling

I keep my tool collection simple and never buy silly gadgets. The more uses I can find for one thing, the better. I tote my hand tools in a Martha Stewart canvas tool bag I got at Kmart for around $20. It's deep, with several pouches on the outside, a couple of pockets inside, and two strong handles. In it I keep the following essential items: a serious hammer; two steel trowels—one wide, one narrow; a claw cultivator for breaking up crusty soil; a curved, foldable pruning saw; a Gertrude Jekyll weeding fork from Hortus Ornamenti in England; a 25-foot Stanley PowerLock tape measure with belt clip; Swiss-made Felco secateurs, the best pruning shears in the world; bonsai scissors, for flower arranging and deadheading; a ball of twine; an old kitchen knife, for disentangling root-bound plants; and a notebook and ink pen. I keep other, less frequently used items in the bag, too, like grass clippers, wire cutters, and an old spoon. And there's plenty of room for a bottle of water, sun screen, herbal insect repellent, and the current issue of *The New Yorker*.

As for large tools, less is more in my garden shed: a heavy iron rake, essential for spreading gravel and soil; a spring rake (fan-shaped, with thin metal tines) for general cleanup and smoothing new seedbeds; a Spear & Jackson border spade from England; its partner, a spading fork, for heavy weeding and turning soil; a sturdy shovel with a pointy blade;

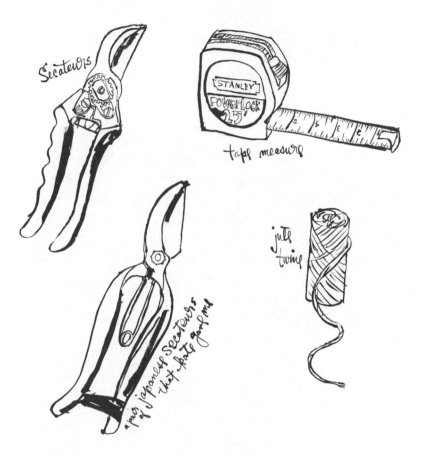

Secateurs

tape measure

jute twine

a pair of Japanese secateurs that feels good but me

an iron pike for dislodging rocks from the soil; and my trusty half-moon edger. Other items include loppers, hedge clippers, and a pick ax. Also in the shed are various galvanized buckets and barrels and a cute broom, for sweeping the paths of the Main Garden. I have no sleek potting bench like all the catalogs try to make you believe you're supposed to have. I use the tailgate of my old Chevy pickup: it's the perfect height, it's portable, and it's easy to hose off and put away.

Buying

I don't do much mail-order shopping for plants, so I've had
to find places in my area that specialize in different things.
I'm extremely picky about the condition of my plants when I
buy them. I've gone into greenhouses rife with aphids and
white flies and walked right out the door. I never buy annuals that are terribly pot-bound; they can be stunted for life.
Pot-bound perennials are a slightly different matter; most
can stand up to serious root surgery, and besides, they can
get on with life in the following year. When considering a
b&b (balled and burlapped) tree or shrub, I grasp the root
ball—not the stem—with both hands and gingerly rock it
from side to side. If it's loose and crumbly, I don't even think
about buying it. When a containerized plant appears to be
pot-bound, I carefully tip it out of its pot when no one is
looking to assess the situation. I reject any woody plant that
has split bark or very blemished and deformed leaves. When
plants, especially annuals, happen to be dry, I request that
they be watered before I buy them. I actually had someone
challenge me on this once. "They're fine," he said, as he
stood with a watering hose in his hand. "They most certainly
are not—not in my book," I countered. He watered them. I
wanted to ask to speak to his boss, but you never know when
someone is having a bad day for a good reason—like maybe
his dog had run away, or his child had had her whole face
pierced. It pays to be considerate. We're all in this together.

Planting

My basic planting method applies to tiny seedlings, towering
trees, and everything in between. (I'm referring here only to

terrestrial plants—ones that anchor themselves in the soil and draw nourishment from it—rather than epiphytes, which dwell in trees, and aquatic plants.) I do most of my planting in spring. When possible, I do it in the early morning, late afternoon, or on cool days so that plants can acclimate before the sun shows up. I never plant in muddy soil; it destroys its texture. I always water plants in their containers before planting them. I remove unhealthy leaves, deadwood, and any weeds, taking extra care when extracting the roots of perennial weeds so that they don't regenerate. If it's a tree or shrub in leaf, I prune only lightly. Removing too much foliage before planting is a mistake; it stresses the plant by reducing its photosynthetic capacity. I dig a five-dollar hole for a half-dollar plant, mix in plenty of manure or compost, and remove the soil from the hole. If the plant is root-bound, I disentangle the roots as much as possible without cutting too many of them. I place the plant in the ground so that the top of the root ball is flush with the top of the hole, then I firm the soil in very well to eliminate air pockets. Then I water twice. I don't tamp or press the wet soil anymore; it creates compaction.

Watering

I once heard a famous gardener say that after something is planted it should never have to be watered again, except by rain. Sorry, that doesn't work for me. Ideally, yes, a new transplant should be so well suited to its situation that it doesn't require babying to get established. I don't coddle a transplant needlessly, but if a spring drought ensues, the last thing I'm going to do is watch it wilt every day. We are usually blessed in this part of the country with ample spring rains, so I do little supplemental watering. And once spring is passed, drought or no drought, plants in the ground are pretty much on their own in my garden. But I'm lucky—I have good natural ground water. So when the soil appears dry at the surface, there is actually moisture down deep that the plants can absorb through osmosis. As for plants in containers, I water them only when needed, and then thoroughly, saturating the soil completely.

Feeding

I wish I could say that I garden totally organically, but I don't. I know I should—it's the right thing to do. I have huge respect for people who are purists in this regard, and I hope to be one myself someday. I never use any kind of chemical herbicides or pesticides, no nasty sprays, but I do use a little synthetic fertilizer. I find it's essential with annuals. Compost and manure, wonderful though they are for conditioning the soil, do not supply sufficient nutrients to these fast-growing plants. With annuals, some perennials, and all container plants, I incorporate a slow-release fertilizer such as Osmocote into the soil at the time of planting. In containers, I also use a diluted liquid fertilizer like Peters throughout the season. I've tried using seaweed and fish emulsion—I like them both—but one time, either the neighbor's cat or some raccoon got a whiff of the fish fertilizer and what it did to my garden three nights in a row nearly put me in the bed. Lately, when planting trees and shrubs, I've stopped using fertilizer. I read a convincing study that said they grow into better plants in the long run when they have to make the best of the soil as is.

Mulching

I'm a big proponent of mulch. It cuts out the light that weed seeds require for germination and also helps stabilize soil moisture and temperature. As it breaks down over time it adds organic matter to the soil, thus enriching it. In the Front Garden, with its trees, shrubs, and herbaceous plants, I sometimes use a fine, ground-up bark mulch, but never those horrible chips or nuggets—too coarse and ugly. Other times I simply mulch the garden with manure or compost, both of which break down more quickly than bark. In the Main Garden, with its annual flowers and summer vegetables, I never use bark; compost or manure gives a country look that's more to my liking. Hay mulch is nice in a vegetable garden, and I've used it, but it doesn't quite suit the Main Garden aesthetically. I mulch the gardens in late spring, after all the planting is done and the volunteers have had a chance to get well established. If possible, I do it right after a good rain, before the soil has a chance to bake.

I know that personal taste is a subjective matter—various types of mulch appeal to different people for different reasons—but how can anyone like that red-orange stuff that's shown up in recent years? I'm afraid to go near it—I'm not even sure what it is. Somebody told me it's dyed cedar. Talk about hideous. There's a McDonald's a few towns away from here (not too near, thank the Lord) with a great sea of the stuff out front, and stranded in it, like lost ships, are six or eight "rug" junipers, flat as pancakes.

Pruning

A plant in the garden deserves to be well shaped. To me, good pruning boils down to three basic elements: sharp tools, timing, and an eye for beauty. For small branches on woody plants I use my Felco secateurs. For larger branches—up to about 4 inches in diameter—I use a curved pruning saw with a 12-inch blade. And when I get into really chunky wood I use a large bow saw. When I prune depends on the nature of the plant being pruned (deciduous or evergreen), its role in the garden, and the desired effect. The only evergreens I have at the moment are boxwoods, which I shear in early spring. I prune spring-flowering trees and shrubs immediately after flowering to shape and manage them; summer-flowering shrubs, like my hydrangea standards, are pruned in late winter. I try to pay attention to a plant's inherent form, and reveal this form through artful pruning. I start by removing any dead or diseased wood, then cut away small, twiggy branches, inward-growing ones, and those that detract from the plant's overall shape. Some plants have poor structure— for example, the ubiquitous Bradford pear, the most over-rated tree in America. It's quite pretty in spring when smothered in white blossoms, but the plant is weak-wooded and its head is a mass of messy sticks. On the other hand, my amelanchier, in the Front Garden, has tremendous grace and beautiful form, which speak to me when I go to prune it.

Composting

When I first came here I threw my fruit and vegetable scraps out in the meadow, well away from the house. I kept a plastic

bucket (still do) on a low shelf in the kitchen and every couple of days I'd dump it. I knew I should be starting a compost
pile, but I kept thinking I had to be very scientific and do
everything just right. One day, I thought, What in the world is
wrong with you—just start piling stuff up. Then I bought a
great little book on composting called *Let It Rot: The Gardener's
Guide to Composting* by Stu Campbell, which was fun to read,
gave a nice overview, and was not too technical. There are all
sorts of details to be concerned with if you wish to be—for
example, the carbon-to-nitrogen ratio—but the bottom line
on composting is in the title of the book: Let it rot.

I have my compost pile behind the tool shed, not far from
the Main Garden. I know people must wonder why I don't
move it, but I rather like the way it looks, and it doesn't
smell bad. I keep it fairly neat by raking the sides upward to
keep if from sprawling everywhere. Every couple of years I
pull it apart and rebuild it. I do this in the fall, after I've cut
down and cleaned up the garden, so that I'll have lots of
bulky stuff to build it with, and because I wouldn't spend my
time in such a way in the hot summertime. I layer the bulky
stuff with the old compost, some manure, and maybe some
hay or straw, and water the layers as I go. I never water it
again and I never turn it. Once in a blue moon, I toss some
lime on it, which contributes calcium and helps with aera-
tion. All year long, even in winter when it's frozen solid and
covered with snow, I dump stuff on it from the kitchen and
garden. In spring, when it thaws out, I use a shovel and rob
from the bottom of the pile, a bucket at a time as needed.
The stuff that comes out is dark and crumbly and smells
sweet and rich.

I love my compost pile. It makes me feel good, because I know I'm doing a good thing for the earth. I figure it balances things karmawise for me, given that I use a little synthetic fertilizer in the garden. One time, when a visitor kept admiring the golden feverfew all over my garden, I gave her a small bag of compost to take home, knowing it was chockful of seeds. Once, when my friend Adele was here from New York City, I was about to dump my compost bucket, and she said, "I want to do it, I want to do it." Compost is elemental.

Weeding

I don't like weeds. A wild plant that's been allowed to inhabit the garden is another matter, but a weed is a weed is a weed. Long ago I got the upper hand on weeds, and now it's a simple matter of maintenance—a necessary habit, like brushing your teeth. Because my garden is small, and because I spend a great deal of time in it, few weeds escape my notice. Mulch helps tremendously, but the little buggers always find a way to get a toehold. One of the last things I do before winter, and one of the first things I do in spring, is it to go round looking for young dandelions and other perennial weeds in the beds and borders. They may look harmless then, but given the chance to gather steam, they will quickly become monsters. While they're small it's a cinch to pop them from the ground, root and all, with my double-pronged Jekyll fork. With annual weeds I don't worry about getting the roots, because they cannot regenerate. It's always tempting to leave a pretty oxalis, and sometimes I do, but it's only asking for trouble: it will flower and set seed in no time.

Tending

I hope my garden doesn't appear too neat, but I like it to look well groomed and presentable. I think the neatness is offset by the lush plantings, the lumpy yard full of clover and violets (my yard is the one place where I like weeds), and the sticks and stones I use to structure the garden with. I groom my plants constantly, because it makes them look lovelier, and because I respect them and honor them for all they give me. Certainly, I don't go overboard, hunting for yellow leaves in out-of-the-way places, but I try to keep plants in prominent places looking their very best.

I love deadheading for the way it brings me into intimate contact with my plants. But increasingly, I find myself choosing things that don't require it, particularly when it comes to annuals. I like some of the short tobaccos very much, like *Nicotiana* 'Domino Lime,' but if they aren't deadheaded daily, they soon look very tatty. Profusion zinnias, whose individual blossoms are very long-lasting, require only minimal deadheading. With annual salvias, such as Lady in Red and Coral Nymph, I let their tall, thin spikes open blossoms for days, then I swoop in and deadhead the whole batch of plants, allowing a mass of fresh spikes to open together. This approach avoids tedious, daily fussing with them.

I tend to stay away from plants that require staking or other support. In the Front Garden especially, I don't want to see sticks or metal cages in the borders. If I can't find a way to support a plant neatly and inconspicuously, I'd rather let it flop—I hate to see a plant looking awkward and strangled. At the rear of the mixed border, I support the

Artemisia lactiflora and *Veronicastrum virginicum,* both of which get tall, by tying them into the hedge. At first I can see the twine, but quite soon it's invisible, covered by leaves. In the Main Garden, I tie gangly sunflowers directly to the stick fence.

The paths in the Main Garden are made of nothing but hard-packed earth and have a baked, adobe-like quality. In certain kinds of light, they look like pink terra-cotta. During a heavy rain, after the ground has reached saturation, water stands in the paths, turning them into canals that reflect the sky. I stand on the porch and marvel at this simply beautiful thing that I could never have anticipated when I was making the garden. The paths drain very quickly after the rain stops, and remarkably, I can walk on them almost immediately—they are not muddy and soft. I love walking barefoot on the paths anytime, but after a rain is best. The combination of warmth and dampness on my feet is utterly delightful. For some reason, this sensation is subtly powerful and makes my garden feel like sacred ground.

One of my favorite garden chores is sweeping the paths, which I do about once a week. I often sweep on Sunday mornings, when I'm expecting visitors, or just because it seems like a good Sunday morning thing to do. I put my coffee cup on a fence post and get to work. I usually sweep the garden in exactly the same way each time, starting at the back and working my way to the front, finishing with four piles of dirt. This might seem extreme and self-conscious, but for me it's become like a spiritual practice. Sweeping the garden makes it appear loved and treasured, which it

most certainly is. Because the paths are so hard-packed, weeds are not a problem. What few sprout along the edges, in the crevices where the stones meet the paths, are easy to pull out while I'm sweeping.

Dirt paths would not work in every garden, but my soil seems to contain just the right amount of clay, which is why the paths look like sun-dried brick. Sweeping the paths repeatedly for ten years has actually caused the garden to sink. When the garden was new, the entrance area was essentially level with the paths; now there is a very noticeable step down. I like this very much—the garden seems to have been pulled into the earth. I see this as a metaphor for my experience with the garden and this place: they have pulled me into them. Sometimes, when I pause from sweeping and look around, I see the garden for a moment as if it were brand new. It's only a small garden of sticks and stones with a swept dirt floor, but it feels like a private, handmade universe.

11. between friends

LIKE MANY PEOPLE, I've learned some of what I know about gardening the hard way, by making mistakes. When I lived on Nantucket and worked for my friend Sonny, I also worked part-time for another gardener, Cindy Collins. Cindy had a slew of clients all over the island for whom she maintained gardens. Nantucket, for anyone who doesn't know it, is situated 22 miles off the southern shore of Cape Cod, Massachusetts, and is only 17 miles long and 4 miles wide. It's a gardener's paradise in many ways, blessed with ocean breezes and bathed in golden light, but it's expensive beyond words and overrun with shiny rich people. It's a cinch to spend $30 on a dinky plate of fish; poor people have to save up for a bar of soap. And forget buying a house—you can't afford one unless you already own two others somewhere else.

Most days while working for Cindy, I supervised a crew of three who went around mowing grass and sprucing up gardens around charming, gray-shingled cottages that were covered in roses and surrounded by privet hedges. It was pleasant work that paid quite well (even a dishwasher makes good money in Nantucket—has to if he's going to afford soap), and while my responsibilities as supervisor were not overwhelming, I was, at the very least, expected to know the basics of lawn maintenance. (I've never taken lawns seriously.)

One spring morning, when everyone had assembled in town, where we always met before dispersing for the day, Cindy informed me that I would be working alone for a change, fertilizing grass. Lovely, I thought. Cindy was a go-getter, up at the crack of dawn, with half a day's work behind her by the time she met up with her sleepy-eyed workers, most of whom were usually hung over. The truck I drove on the job, which belonged to Cindy, was already loaded up with several bags of nitrogen-rich fertilizer and a two-wheeled calibrated spreader that you pushed like a baby carriage. As I got into the truck and waved good-bye to the others, I thought, Aren't you just somebody important.

I don't remember exactly where I began with the fertilizing, but I do remember having a long list of places I was supposed to visit by day's end. Chances are I went first to Quidnet, a tiny settlement midway between the town of Nantucket and Siasconset, a picturesque village on the eastern end of the island that everyone called Sconset. Of all the gardens my crew and I tended, my favorite was in Quidnet. The small house it went with sat on a hilltop, engulfed by a fat, balloon-like hedge. Inside the hedge was a sweet dooryard garden, where rambling flower borders surrounded a perfect patch of green grass, a great place to sit or stroll and enjoy the colorful flowers. The whole package, ocean view and all, was like something out of a storybook with a happy ending.

After a quick gander at the garden and a few snoopy minutes of peering into windows (nobody was home), I unloaded the spreader and a bag of fertilizer from the truck. "You *have* done this before, haven't you?" Cindy had asked that morning. I lied that I had. "Great, the instructions are on the bag for how much to use." Then she told me where to find her if I finished early. Fat chance, I thought, staring at my list.

Fertilizer is heavy. I'm a strong man, so the weight of the bags wasn't a problem per se, but I found them to be cumbersome. Right off the bat, in the Quidnet garden, I spilled a bunch of fertilizer on the perfect green grass as I was pouring it into the spreader. Not to worry, I thought, as I brushed the granules into the turf. All day long, I kept spilling piles of the stinky fertilizer in people's yards. Also, from the first, I had decided that either the instructions on the bag were wrong or the spreader wasn't working properly: what else could explain the trickle of stuff coming out that looked so insufficient? All day long, I tripled the amount of fertilizer I applied.

When I saw Cindy at the end of the day she seemed a tad peeved that I hadn't finished in time to join up with her and the others, and she was clearly disappointed that I hadn't got round to all the gardens on my list. She also appeared shocked at the amount of fertilizer I had used. When I confidently informed her of what I had done, her eyes widened: "How much extra?" she asked, with dread in her voice. "Oh, I'd say I went over everything at least three times," I replied, suddenly feeling very small. The conversation ended without my mentioning the spillage.

This happened to be a Friday, and that night, unable to get the look on Cindy's face out of my mind, I called my friend Sonny to get his opinion on what I had done. Sonny was his usual low-key self, but the more I talked, the more he felt it would be a good idea to take a look at some of the yards. As it was springtime, the majority of Nantucket's summer people were not yet in residence, so we knew it would be safe to prowl around the gardens. Sonny picked me up early Saturday morning and off we went to investigate.

Horrors! I had made big messes almost everywhere I had been. One of the worst was in a garden in Wauwinet (Nantucket has lots of Indian place names). The large lawn was dotted with bright yellow blobs where spilled fertilizer had burned into the turf. At a place on Polpis Harbor, in a front yard that rolled down to the water, the grass was striped with wide yellow bands. In the garden in Quidnet there was the biggest, ugliest blob of all, just where you stepped through the gate and onto the patch of grass. When I held my hand over it I could actually feel the heat. How could I not have known how powerful the concentrated fertilizer was? I must have slept through Turf Management class in school.

Sonny said somebody needed to get water on those lawns fast, to dilute the fertilizer, and suggested I call Cindy and tell her what we had seen. I tried to get up my nerve but chickened out. Hope for the best and plan for the worst, I thought. (What can I say? I was still a kid.) Monday morning came painfully fast. The moment I saw Cindy she shot me a look that told me she knew all about the blobs and stripes. Poor thing, she had spent her whole weekend running around like mad, setting up sprinklers in an effort to save the grass. Most of the stripes eventually disappeared, thanks to Cindy's watering. But the blobs, one and all, had to be dug up and replaced with sod. I felt awful. To this day I've never bought a bag of lawn fertilizer. But as I said, I don't take lawns seriously. Too bad I didn't tell Cindy that in the first place, instead of jumping into the truck with the fertilizer and zooming off like a smarty-pants.

We never stop making mistakes—at least I don't—but fortunately, by the time I moved to the Catskills a few years later to start making a garden for my friend Kate Pierson, I had grown up a lot and stopped doing things like burning grass and not telling the boss. I met Kate when I first moved to New York City in the mid-1980s, and the moment we met, at a Christmas Eve party, we started talking gardens. She had been a serious organic gardener when she lived in Athens, Georgia, where she and the other members of the B-52's had met and formed their band. Since moving to New York she had missed her garden hugely and was excited that night about a house she had just bought upstate, in Woodstock. "I would love you to come help me start a garden there someday," Kate said.

Four years later, in May 1990, I did just that. Kate, who was planning to be away on a concert tour for the entire summer, offered me her house to live in. (It wasn't until the following year that I found my own place.) Built in the late 1930s, her Adirondack-style cabin faced a pond and sat at the upper end of a gently sloping, wooded 3-acre property. I was thrilled to be gardening for the first time since leaving Nantucket, and it felt great to have something serious to sink my teeth into.

Kate Pierson: a Cosmic thing—among the Cosmos

Near the house, beautiful trees—paper birch and red oak—and native shrubs—highbush blueberry and winterberry holly—were being swallowed up by the encroaching woods. I hired a man to thin and prune the trees, and I pruned and shaped the shrubs myself. To skirt the house and connect it with the stony landscape, I began constructing low walls to contain planting beds, from fieldstone I gathered on the property. This was the first of a lot of stonework I would do on the property over the years, and I was pleased with the look of my walls. Since coming to the Catskills I had noticed the abundance of old stone walls that laced the countryside; everywhere I went, I observed how they were constructed. I didn't care much for the ones made of thin, cut bluestone. I much preferred the rustic, organic look of rough fieldstone. It was very satisfying to search through the woods and down by the pond for shapely stones for my walls.

Kate and I had not had much time to discuss the design of her garden, so I was left to my own devices. I appreciated the freedom she had given me, but it was overwhelming, too. The biggest mistake I made at Kate's was to not carefully consider every aspect, particularly the exterior, of the house. The front of the house, which jutted into the woods, featured a wide porch. One of the beds I had made ran parallel to the porch for its entire width. It was in scale with the house and had good proportions, and it made a fine place for shade-loving plants, but it should have been interrupted in the middle by stone steps, centered on the door to the house and leading down into the woods. In hindsight, my mistake seems so obvious, but at the time, I merrily went about my work like a person hanging laundry in the rain.

In midsummer I decided to build a long 60-foot stone walk down the middle of the yard, to connect the house with the driveway. I tracked Kate down in Australia and discussed my idea with her briefly. It was hard for her to focus, and I could tell she had reservations, but in the end she said to go for it if it seemed like the right thing to do.

At first I was planning to simply shave off the turf, collect a bunch of good-looking flat stones from the woods, and get on with it. But a few days before I began work, I was telling a new friend, a local guy, about my idea. He said that I should first dig down in the ground a few inches and lay in a thick layer of stone dust—to absorb moisture and prevent the walk from heaving during winter's freezing and thawing—before putting down the flat paving stones. He also said, in a polite way, that I was crazy if I went collecting all that stone myself, because I could buy plenty of it, and a pile of stone dust, too, from a stone yard and have it delivered and dumped right where I needed it. (I had never thought of paying for rocks before.) I said, "Okay, buddy, I hear you talking. I appreciate your advice."

The next thing I knew, I was out there with a pick ax and shovel, digging up the ground. Much of the soil in the Catskills (my own being a delightful exception) is poor and junky. Unlike the southern Appalachians and the Rockies, both of which actually rose up out of the earth, the Catskill Mountains were formed from an eroded plateau. It was easy to see the result of this in Kate's soil, which was filled with shale, a fine-grained, thinly bedded rock that splits easily. One of the main reasons I had begun making raised beds was so that I could fill them with good soil. Shale, for anyone who doesn't know it, is hateful stuff—it gets in your way constantly, banging stubbornly against your spade when you try to plunge it into the ground. It's enough to turn a sane human crazy, and it almost did me, when I began to dig up the ground for the walk.

I was out there for *days* digging that mess up, a few chunks at a time, cussing and moaning and feeling like the last slave in Egypt. One day, when I was still less than half-finished, the friendly local guy dropped by to say hey. "What are you *doing?*" he asked, his eyes bulging from his head as he looked at me standing calf-deep in the ground. I said, "Well, what in the world does it look like I'm doing? I'm digging these fool rocks out of here just like you told me to do, and it's about to put me in an early grave." Shaking his head, he said, "I didn't mean that you should do it with your hands. I can't believe you've done

all this. Now put those tools away. I'll be back here tomorrow."

Bright and early the next morning, he came rolling down
the driveway like a knight in shining armor, with a cute little
backhoe on the bed of his monster truck. And before I had
time to properly say good morning, he had that magic
machine on the ground and was scooping up that junky soil
like somebody eating ice cream. I thought, Dean, you need
your head examined—*bad.*

After that I hired a professional stonemason to finish the
walk. But here's the punch line: Would you believe we had
that silly walk taken up a few years later? Kate had the driveway moved, and when she did, the walk no longer made
any sense. Actually, it should never have been put there to
begin with: it cut the yard in half and had no logical relationship to the overall landscape. Kate was just as sweet as
she could be about my big flub and never once made me
feel like a jerk. Meanwhile, I felt like a body without a brain
in it.

Over time, I concentrated my efforts and Kate's money
on the enclosed kitchen garden we made in the second
year, and let most of the property stay wild and untamed.
Kate sold her house recently and moved into one that she
had built nearby, where there are lots of possibilities for new
gardens. Our friends Jeffrey and Dominic bought her old
house, and Dominic took to the garden instantly. It's awfully
nice, after all those years of hard work, to see that not just
someone, but a friend, has come along who cares about and
delights in the garden. He got a taste of the good life right
away, when a groundhog got in the garden in spring and ate

up some of his newly planted vegetables. Like all good gardeners, he whined about it briefly, then rose above it. In no time he had beans and peas coming out of his ears and dahlias for days.

I don't make gardens for other people as much as I used to, and when I do I prefer small projects. I'm very hands-on and there are only so many hours in the day. With small gardens I can do most of the work myself and have a lot of control over the results. This is one of the reasons I've so enjoyed the tiny storefront garden in nearby Phoenicia that I made a few years ago.

The shop, called The Tender Land, is run by my friend Bill and sells gifts and home accessories. Bill has a great eye—the shop is smart and sophisticated without being exclusive or overpriced. It's perfect for little old Phoenicia, a place nobody wants to see turn into anything other than just what it is, an unpretentious, country town of everyday people. I love it. Just the other day, in the early evening, I went to town to check on the garden. As I was strolling down the sidewalk, nodding and speaking to familiar people, I said to myself, This is wonderful. I love my adopted town. On the rare occasions when I find myself trapped in nightmarish suburban traffic, I think about Phoenicia and instantly feel better. There's not a Wal-Mart, a CVS, or even a traffic light for miles around. A person can breathe and know he's alive.

Bill's garden consists of two square raised beds, 8 feet by 8 feet, bisected by a stone walk that leads to the door of the shop. The beds are edged with river stones I collected up the road. In the middle of each bed is a Korean tree lilac, and marking each corner is a boxwood ball (*Buxus* 'Green Gem'). The rest of the planting changes completely twice a year: tulips and other bulbs for spring and annuals for summer. A few times I've planted mums and ornamental cabbages for the fall, but usually the summer planting is presentable enough until mid-October to let it suffice. Besides, by October I'm ready to yank it all out, plant the bulbs for next year, and call it a season.

I've been tempted at times to convert the garden to perennials to make things easier. This idea usually hits me in springtime, when I've got so much on my plate. But I've concluded it's simply not the place for it: being such a small garden and visible to so many people, it's the perfect place for seasonal bedding, which keeps things more interesting for all concerned. Much like Bill's shop, where the merchandise constantly changes, his garden picture changes too, while the frame (the bone structure) remains the same. I've had people in town be kind enough to admire the garden in my presence, saying that what they like most about it is that "it's always different." Bill's garden is a marvelous place to experiment with color and texture, and as the garden is situated in full sun, plant choices are virtually unlimited.

Every autumn I plant a different variety of tulips. The following spring, when they've finished flowering, the plants come out, bulbs and all. Some people find this wasteful, but the plants get composted, which is a worthy end for them. Besides, buying new bulbs every year is good for business at Brent and Becky's Bulbs, in Gloucester, Virginia, which is where I usually order my tulips from.

When I plant, I really pack in the bulbs, at least a hundred in each bed. I toss them over the beds, let them fall where they may, fiddle with them a bit, then sink them with a hand-driven bulb planter. Some I plant singly, others I group into threes or fives and plant together in masses. This is pleasant work, as Bill's soil is loose and crumbly—a tad dry in high summer, but this is offset by its richness. A couple of years ago I added grape hyacinth bulbs (*Muscari armeniacum*) among the tulips. They don't always flower exactly at the same moment, depending on the variety of tulip, but there is usually enough of an overlap to make this an effective spring combination. Unlike the tulips, the muscari are treated as perennials, but their unsightly, withering foliage, which must be allowed to ripen and nourish the bulbs, is soon covered up by the burgeoning summer annuals.

Last May, the garden was filled with Spring Green tulips, a viridiflora type described in Brent and Becky's catalog as having "lovely ivory petals with apple-green feathered flames; as fresh as a new spring day." Well said. I often underplant the emerging tulips with leaf lettuce, as soon as I can find some good plants for sale. Sometimes I simply dot them informally through the beds; other times I create patterns that play off the garden's geometry. Not only does the lettuce make a good companion to the tulips, but it also puts fresh salad on my table and Bill's much earlier than my own garden, which doesn't warm up as fast as Bill's in spring. I love to pick lettuce and walk right over to the German deli across the street and give it to Margaret, the owner. One day she insisted on giving me a chocolate bar, which had delicious gooey cherries in it. Margaret makes snapshots of the tulips every year and puts them in an album. This touches me.

For the summer show I make tapestry plantings, like those in my Inner Garden at home. The two beds are planted with the same selection of annuals, but because the plants are arranged differently in each bed, they both have their own look. This is such a fun way to play with plant form and habit. The geometric structure of the garden anchors the whole picture and gives it definition.

This year I combined yellow signet marigolds (*Tagetes tenuifolium* 'Lemon Gem') with *Petunia integrifolia* 'Alba,' trailing blue scaevola (*S.* 'Blue Wonder'), *Salvia* 'White Nymph,' and a jazzy coleus called Kiwi Fern, which has burgundy foliage tipped with cream and green. At the center of each bed, around the lilac standards, I planted large, bushy plectranthuses (*Plectranthus cilatus*) with showy, ruffled leaves of green and white. Popping out of the stone edges and dotted all through is golden feverfew and *Verbena bonariensis*. As I write, it's late July and the planting looks rather good, I don't mind saying.

I know I go on endlessly about *Petunia integrifolia* 'Alba,' but it really is the most marvelous plant—it's so clean and fresh-looking and has such an excellent growth habit. It has romped delightfully into the yellow marigolds, among their ferny, scented leaves and small single blossoms. The blue scaevola, another rambler, has flowers that look like little fans. It, too, has shot through everything, and looks especially good with the burgundy coleus. I once wrote something awful about scaevola in my column, "Dean's Dirt," in *Elle Décor* magazine. I said that it was "dull, dull, dull." I can't imagine what possessed me to say such a thing. I take it all back. Scaevola is absolutely fabulous. It flowers like mad for weeks and weeks, requires no deadheading, and is anything but dull, dull, dull.

Bill seems as pleased as I am with the garden this year. One day, as we stood together admiring it, I was suddenly hit with an idea for next year. "Why not use all the same kinds of plants, but in hot colors?" I asked. Then I zipped through the list: orange signet marigolds, magenta petunias (*P. integrifolia*, the straight species), Lady in Red salvia, blue scaevola (yes, I know blue is a cool color), gray-leafed plectranthus (*P. argentatus*), and Garnet Robe, a trailing coleus with velvet maroon leaves. "Sounds like Mexico," said Bill. Sounds like a party to me.

As for next year's tulips, I'm thinking Sweet Harmony, a single late tulip with pale, pale yellow blossoms that I grew in my garden years ago. They would look wonderful with the blue muscari, and perhaps some red oak-leaf lettuce scattered about.

Much as I love Phoenicia, I'm thoroughly put out with somebody: there's a thief in our midst! That's right, a low-down plant robber. The other day Bill called to say that two plectranthuses had been stolen from one of the beds. I hit the roof. It's bad enough when people break off plants for their own amusement or toss cigarette butts and bits of paper into the garden. That I can live with. But stealing from a flower garden is simply beyond the pale, and really quite tacky when you think about it. Had it been a hungry person stealing vegetables, it would have been a different matter. But two frilly plants with variegated leaves? I'm sorry, there is no forgiving it. Not only did the vile individual do something immoral and illegal, he also did a very selfish thing: "Oh, I'll just take these plants for wonderful, deserving me and let everyone else suffer."

I immediately made an attractive cardboard sign, drove into town, and erected it in the garden. It read as follows: "Dear Phoenicia, For the second time (the first was two years ago) some thoughtless, low-class person has stolen two large plants from this garden. If anyone knows who the nasty, wretched culprit is, please call The Tender Land. This small garden is for everyone's enjoyment. HELP US GET THE THIEF! Many thanks, the gardener."

Of course, no one ever called. I finally took the sign down because I was sick of looking at it, but it was cathartic for a few days. At first, I found myself hoping that the stolen plants would die. Then I thought, No, I hope they live and thrive so that the criminal can be reminded daily of his awful deed. I can't help but think that the dirty dog in question is the same person who stole plants two years ago: in both cases, the plants were taken from the same bed in exactly the same place. Last time, it was purple fountain grass. I fantasized later that the crook would slice his hands on the sharp-edged leaf blades. This time, I'm hoping that he has an allergy to plectranthus and that his horrible thieving paws have broken out in a painful rash. I know I'm being ugly, but now you've seen my dark side.

 on the porch

I HAVE EIGHTEEN SMOOTH PEBBLES that I collected on
the beach a few years ago during a trip to Sag Harbor on
Long Island, where my friend Ricks lives. The pebbles vary
in shape, size, and color. I have them arranged on a chartreuse Russel Wright plate and on display in the screened
front porch, on the bottom shelf of an old sewing box that I
got for $3 at a yard sale. Occasionally, I pick up the plate
and observe the pebbles in detail, and I remember the
windy summer day when I collected them. I was with Ricks,
and I can see his blond hair blowing in the wind, as he lis-
tens to me talk about the pebbles in my hands. Ella, Ricks's
black-and-white dog, is playing in the sand. I can almost
smell the sea air. This triggered evocation, this picture of a
day spent with a friend I dearly love, a friend I see too little

of, is why I keep eighteen beautiful pebbles displayed on my porch. I am always aware of them, and because they mean so much to me, I regularly wash them and the plate they sit on. Even the plate has significance: it was part of a collection of Russel Wright dishes that my friend Barry gave me.

The longer I live, the more I dislike excess belongings: they get in the way of really seeing and appreciating necessary possessions or ones with special meaning, like my pebbles. My porch is small. I like it to be comfortable and inviting, but not cluttered. All the furniture I have, I bought cheaply or found abandoned. The few items that I use for decoration are mainly treasured family heirlooms that have little or no monetary value. I used to think the porch needed to be gussied up—you know, little darling things put around—but something always kept me from it, and now I know why: the essence of a space with naturally good atmosphere is spoiled by overembellishment. Similarly, I've found that owning too many things, period, is spiritually burdensome: it spoils the atmosphere of my soul.

I love things that tell a story or stir something in me when I look at them. Hanging on the wall of my porch, over a metal chair, is a glass painting of the U.S. Capitol building. The painting, in a dark wooden frame, belonged to my paternal grandmother and hung for years in the house where she lived with my aunt and uncle. When I pause to look at it, countless sights, sounds, and smells flood over me, and I'm a child again, in "Granny's side" of the house. Frankly, the painting itself is about shot; half the paint has flaked away from the glass, leaving much of the cardboard backing visible. But there is no mistaking the famous building. I think the condition of the painting is a perfect metaphor for the appalling state of things in Washington, D.C.

On the wall a few feet away, beside a window that looks into the living room, is a green enamel dishpan that came from my Uncle Roy's boyhood home. It's a wonderful piece, sturdy and deep, and in the bottom someone mended two holes with tiny nuts and screws. I don't use the pan often—it simply hangs on the red wall to please my eye. But occasionally, when there are lots of people to feed, I use it in the yard to wash up a mess of greens from the garden. I'm always amazed that it doesn't leak around the screws. Who mended the pan? Was it my Uncle Roy, or was he still a child at the time?

When I first moved into my house it was summertime and I went almost daily to the creek across the road, to cool off in the water or simply take in the beauty of my new surroundings. In the field between my house and the creek there was a huge pile of rubbish. It's since been cleaned up, thank the Lord, but at the time it was simply disgraceful. It looked like somebody had taken a house trailer, turned it upside down, and shaken out the contents. I could hardly bare to look at it, but one day my curiosity got the best of me, so I started prowling through it. At first,

five dollar Chair

all I found worth keeping was an old peach basket. But then I saw part of a small wooden table sticking up. It turned out to be good-looking, so I hauled it home and cleaned it up, and it's been with me ever since. It's what you might call a "farm table," plain as it can be, well made, and just right for my porch. I never stop admiring it. If I went shopping in Paris I wouldn't be able to find a table that suits my porch as well.

I have another good table on the porch—a larger, taller one, which I got for ten bucks at a junk store in Hunter, when my friend Ken and I were knocking around the mountaintop one day. Somebody told me it's called a "trestle table." It has two fat legs shaped like fancy A's with a bar connecting them at the bottom. It's obviously been painted and repainted many times. I sanded it just enough to make

it smooth, so that plenty of color would still show through—
gray, red, black, yellow, white, and a lot of green. It makes a
fine buffet table for summer dinner parties, and it's great
for resting groceries on when I step onto the porch. It's also
where I do my flower arranging.

I like an arrangement to tell a story of a plant and a container. I want the flower to tell the plant's story of grace,
form, and beauty. In other words, I want it to speak for
itself. For this reason, I like simple, uncomplicated arrangements composed of just one kind of flower. Sometimes, in
my small house, all that's needed to bring the garden
indoors is one blossom. Of course, there are exceptions, but
arrangements that include many different things are often
overwrought and uninspiring. If they are done with awareness and sensitivity it's one thing, but this seems rarely to be
the case.

Recently, while dining with two friends in a New York
restaurant, my companions noticed a large arrangement at
the front of the dining room. While they ugired that the
ingredients themselves were quite lovely, they could not settle on what it was about the whole composition that was
unsatisfactory. For some reason, I didn't offer an opinion,
but I could see the problem at a glance: everything fought. I
mean, red Japanese maple leaves with lilies and larkspurs? I
don't think so. It's so easy to gild the lily, so to speak, and so
disastrous in the end. The maple branches alone would
have been elegant and sophisticated.

It never ceases to amaze me how many tired flower
arrangements you see in restaurants. Every detail in the
place will appear to be attended to, and yet perched in the

most obvious place of all will be a great, stiff wad of out-of-season flowers in a vase of dirty water. Why bother at all? It's absolutely fine—preferable—to not have cut flowers or plants in a restaurant unless they are going to be presented with flair and taste. Or at the very least, in clean water. When I sit down at a table in a restaurant, I notice everything about it. If flowers are part of the setting and happen to be fresh and well arranged, I start to get a good feeling about the quality of the food and the cleanliness of the kitchen.

I was on a press trip to Pennsylvania last winter that included lunch at Simon Pearce, on the banks of the Brandywine River. The moment we stepped into the simple dining room we were greeted warmly, and I got a sense that something special lay ahead. When we were shown to our table, I was delighted to see that it was flawless and sparsely set. At the center of the table was a single, red gerbera daisy in a sparkling-clean glass vase. I'm not especially fond of gerbera daisies, but this is not the point. The point is that someone cared enough about his or her job to do it extremely well. And that someone obviously had a like-minded associate in the kitchen: lunch, in a word, was superb.

I have a small assortment of vases, jugs, jars, and pitchers that I use for flowers. Most of them have great sentimental value. A few belonged to my mother and grandmothers, some were gifts from friends, and still others I picked up during trips away from home. I don't travel a great deal, so when I go somewhere special, I like to return with an inexpensive memento. As with pots and containers for the garden, I don't add to my collection arbitrarily or often.

I love a good pitcher. Perhaps it's the intended use of the vessel—to fill and replenish—that makes it seem so appropriate for a flower arrangement: a good arrangement should pleasure the eyes and fill a person with inspiration. I was very drawn to a small glass pitcher while lunching at Simon Pearce. Simon Pearce is a group of artisans who make superb blown-glass and pottery. Next to the lovely restaurant is a shop where you can purchase their goods, and one whole section is devoted to seconds. Seconds are my favorites—I love the perfection of imperfection when it comes to decorative objects. I saw a short, square pitcher with a crooked spout and a crooked handle and lots of tiny bubbles in the clear glass. Sadly, at $35, the little darling-didn't fall into the category of "inexpensive memento"—not that day anyway. I can still see that thing in my life with a sprig of forget-me-nots in it. Good excuse for a trip back to Brandywine country.

One of my favorite ceramic pitchers was a gift from my friend Barbara. It's green, squat, and rounded, white inside, with a touch of yellow at the rim. It's not a fine piece, nor is it rare, but it has excellent lines and its apple green color is fresh and playful. I use it in July to fea-  ture the blossoms of *Clematis* 'Niobe,' which are the color of ruby port. Not all clematises are good as cut flowers, but Niobe is quite long lasting. I drape them broadly over the pitcher, and always include a leaf or two, which are very attractive and add greatly to

Barbara's pitcher

the composition. The pitcher is also lovely filled with magenta gomphrena.

I have a Blue Ridge Pottery pitcher that belonged to my maternal grandmother, Granny Hudson. One look at it and I'm on her back porch in Laurens, South Carolina, where a roll-top hutch sitting to one side contained all sorts of kitchen items, including the pitcher I now treasure. It came to Mama when Granny died, and she gave it to me the first time I left home to "set up housekeeping." I wouldn't trade it for the world. I rarely use it for anything but clean white hydrangea blossoms. Something very colorful would compete with the hand-painted pitcher, which is decorated with apples, grapes, pears, and plums. I hope Granny knows in heaven how much I love her pitcher. Lord, what I wouldn't give today to sit with her at her kitchen table and dunk toast in coffee. I'd give her pitcher, that's what I'd give.

Sometimes it's fun to be, oh, not silly, but a bit childish when arranging flowers. Years ago I wouldn't have been caught dead growing marigolds. But now I love them in the vegetable garden. I usually stick to the tiny-flowered Gem

series, but this year I also planted Disco Flame, which is short and bushy with single blooms of red and yellow. And for the first time ever I planted some big double ones (*Tagetes* 'Antigua Orange'). They're just a kick to have around. The other day I put one fat blossom—as orange as I don't know what and big as a mountain—in a dark gray Russel Wright cream pitcher. What was so fun about it was the way the flower just sat there like a bump on a log, screaming.

Of course, subtlety is always in order, too. My swamp azaleas in the Front Garden were loaded with scented blooms this year, pure white and sweet like jasmine. I use to see this species, one of the many deciduous azaleas native to the eastern United States, all over Nantucket, which is one reason I grow it. It grows in wet ground in the wild, but it's quite happy in my garden in well-drained soil. One July day I cut a sprig of the azalea and placed it in a small glass jug that my friend Anne brought me from London. "I've got something for you I think you're going to like," she had said to me in a note. And she was absolutely right.

I threw out most of the bottle collection years ago that I had as a teenager, but I kept a few things. One is an old-fashioned milk bottle—the kind that, before my time, the milkman left at your door. Printed on the bottle in red letters is the following: "PET Pasteurized Milk Grade A Laboratory Controlled." And on the other side: "Taste the Fresh Cream in Pet Ice Cream 'a health food.' " Pet was, and still is, a common brand of dairy products in some parts of the South. I don't use the milk bottle often, but when I do, it looks good on my kitchen windowsill with a sunflower sticking out of it. And it reminds me of the day I discovered it, buried in the ground on my brother-in-law's farm.

I don't care for extravagant gift giving, partly because I can't afford to give extravagantly, but mostly because it's so unnecessary. The best gifts are simple ones with thought behind them. My friends Roger and Eduardo excel in this department. One year for Christmas they gave me some maple syrup—not much, just enough for a few stacks of pancakes. But the bottle it came in was special. They had taken an old medicine bottle and attached a homemade label to it. I don't know what kind of glue they used, but the label, which has the impression of a pressed maple leaf on it, has never peeled away even slightly. The bottle is sitting on my desk now, with a lone white zinnia in it. One thing I find so worthwhile about a single blossom placed on my desk, or kitchen windowsill, or by the telephone, is that I am more apt to notice and enjoy its marvelous subtleties, than when I'm out in the garden, where so much is going on. When I cut the White Profusion zinnia the other day and put it in the bottle, I saw for the first time that the undersides of its petals are tipped with spring green, as though the creator decided to paint them at the last minute.

My most treasured container of all for cut flowers is a white McCoy vase that belonged to my mother. I liked it fine when I was growing up but never thought much about it. It was just there. A few times Mama put some plastic red poinsettias in it at Christmastime. Eventually, it wound up in the laundry room—which we called "the little room"—on a shelf over the dryer. When Mama was sick with terminal cancer, I used to see it when I'd do laundry and feel guilty for wanting it. Occasionally, I use it for dahlias, hydrangeas, or peonies, but it was *made* for sunflowers. It sits about 8 inches tall, with a fat base that tapers to the neck then flares slightly at the mouth. Something about the shape and size of the vase, and its creamy white color, enhances a bouquet of sunflowers like nothing I've ever seen. And the flowers do the same for the vase. A successful arrangement depends largely on a complementary relationship between the container and its contents. The only difficulty with this arrangement is getting the top-heavy sunflowers to behave—they want to flop over the sides too much. I take a stout, twiggy branch from a deciduous shrub and force it gently down into the vase. This creates a support system in which to intersperse the flower stems and hold them upright.

I once made a flower arrangement in June in the south of France. This was more than twelve years ago, and I was there for a week with my employer at the time, an American garden designer who had a client, an American billionaire, who owned a house in Provence. Periodically, the client—I'll call her Mrs. White—would fly the designer—I'll call him John—to France on the Concorde, to help her "refine" her garden. John always took an assistant along on these fantastic trips, and during the short time I worked for him, I lucked out. Hot dog! (Stay tuned for more on the flower arrangement—I'll make it worth the wait.)

Like a fool, the night before John and I left for France, I went out in New York and got smashed. When Mrs. White's driver picked us up at her apartment in Manhattan to take us to Kennedy Airport, I felt like death warmed over and then some. We happened to be charged with taking Mrs. White's two dogs—both of whom had reserved seats on the Concorde—with us to France, where she would be joining us in a couple of days. One dog was a friendly, spaniel-like mutt; the other one was stuck up and looked like a dust mop. I wound up with the mop. Mere moments after the jet took off like a rocket, a stunning flight attendant came round, smiled a French smile, and placed a bowl of water on the seatback tray for the dog. Miss Mop turned up her nose—she was used to the Concorde. Next, the flight attendant offered me a tall, thin, ice-cold glass of vodka, which I gladly accepted—I *wasn't* used to the Concorde. I thought, Child, you're in some high cotton now if you never were before. I sipped the elixir, melted into my seat, and looked across the aisle at Henry Kissinger. Scary.

The house was beyond fabulous. And yet, it was understated—my favorite kind of fabulous. It wasn't enormous. It wasn't even big by some standards. But it was tremendous. It was old and mellow and comfortable and perfect, and there were servants—oodles of them—and swags of jasmine in flower over the front door, and great, soaring Italian cypresses, and fields of lavender and rosemary, and a potager and cutting garden, and a vineyard, and yes, olive trees with wildflowers underneath, and a sweeping view of the countryside. And light. Oh, my heavenly days, the light that fell on that gentle place was out of this world. I can't begin to do the place justice.

To top things off, there was a miracle in the kitchen—a French chef who turned out the best food I've ever put in my mouth. I do not exaggerate in the least when I say that every morsel put before me throughout the week was absolutely sublime. It seemed that every time I turned around we were sitting down on what Mrs. White called the "sunset terrace," to another meal from the magic hands of you know who. Our hostess appeared to have a major fondness for truffles, because they seemed to show up in some form or other at almost every meal. Fine with me—how often did I eat velvet omelets studded with shards of black truffle?

There were two other houseguests present that week: an odd pair, not a married couple, from London. The man, an antiques dealer, looked sort of like an English Liberace—

not nearly so over-the-top, but done up. His dyed black hair was never out of place and it looked as if it had been polished. The woman, who wore lots of yellow and had sculpted, silvery hair, looked like a paper-doll cutout, and spoke without parting her teeth. I noted this particularly at lunch one day, when, for a reason I can't recall, she began talking about how she never ate corn on the cob, because she could not bear for the kernels to get stuck in her teeth. She delivered this without a trace of humor in her voice, as though she were imparting some great (I can't resist) kernel of wisdom.

Frankly, I don't remember doing much work. Oh, I clipped a viburnum hedge once for a minute or two, and styled some flower pots around the pool house for a photo shoot that was to take place while we were there. But otherwise it was just one soft and golden day after another. One day, John asked me to cut some flowers and make an arrangement for a small sitting room in the house. He took me to a room off the kitchen that contained shelf after shelf of china, glassware, and every kind of vessel for arranging flowers in that you could imagine. He selected a clunky, ceramic jug and shoved it at me. I promptly rejected it. I said, "If you want me to do the arrangement, let me to do it my way. I'd like to go and spend a few minutes in the room and decide for myself which container to use." He said, "Fine, I respect that."

The room, whose colors were mainly pastel, was what I'd call a parlor—not that I'm often in one. It was pretty, feminine without being fussy, and personal. I seem to remember some pictures of Mrs. White's children. There were lovely, small paintings on the walls, old books on tables, several ornamental chairs, and a proper settee. I felt the room called for a light, airy arrangement in a very simple container.

Back in the china room, I found a short crystal vase with a nice flared mouth. In the garden I cut blue nigella, pink columbine, white baby's breath, and pale, pale yellow scabiosa. Everything was lacy and sweet. I filled the vase two-thirds full of water, then worked on the arrangement until the position of every leaf, blossom, and stem was to my liking. Then I remembered the white jasmine over the front door. I went and clipped a single sprig of the perfumed vine and added it to my composition, allowing it to spill down the side of the vase. I placed the flowers on a table in the sitting room, and went in search of John. When he saw the arrangement, he loved it, which delighted me. Later, after Mrs. White had seen it, John told me that she had been "thrilled over it."

On Saturday night, Mrs. White gave a dinner party for ten or twelve people. Around seven o'clock the guests began to arrive and assemble on the sunset terrace for drinks and hors d'oeuvres. From the terrace, one looked down on a small field of lavender, bisected by a wide gravel path that was edged with big rosemary bushes and led to the potager and cutting garden. Beyond the gardens, the green-and-white Provençal countryside stretched to the horizon. I'll never forget holding my glass of rosé up to the sunset to see the light swim in the pale pink liquid.

Among the invited guests were Sir Stephen Spender, the famous English poet and author, and his wife, Lady Natasha.

The couple owned a house a few miles away. Sir Stephen and I hit it off immediately. I had never read his writing, but I knew enough about the man to be aware of his past association with his compatriot writers, W. H. Auden and Christopher Isherwood, both of whom were deceased. I was dying to ask about them, but I didn't dare—it would have been gauche. I'm so glad I didn't, because when I asked about his "work," he politely said, "Oh, I never talk about my work. Why don't *you* tell me more about growing up in South Carolina?"

Mrs. White, a very poised, attractive woman in her sixties, did not appear until all the guests had arrived. At last, she emerged from the house and floated across the emerald lawn—which was striped with long, dramatic shadows cast by the tall cypress trees—in a breezy, drop-dead-gorgeous celery-and-cantaloupe gown. As she approached the group, all conversation dwindled to a murmur, then stopped. Everyone turned to face her. What an entrance. Later, the housekeeper told me that the gown was Moschino couture.

After a dinner of pink, juicy lamb and baby root vegetables, followed by raspberry soufflé that was like something out of a dream, we retired to a large drawing room for coffee, brandy, and more conversation. Unlike the earlier sitting room, this one had a slightly masculine feeling. The colors were warm, the sofas and chairs were deep, and the fabrics were rich and sumptuous. Everyone mingled and played musical chairs to the tune of brandy, as Mrs. White passed a guest book around. (I'd pay to see what I wrote.)

At one point, John and I wound up sitting with Stephen and Natasha, just the four of us. John was famous for hogging the floor, and that night was no exception. But the Spenders were a picture of tolerance and good manners, smiling and nodding at every word he said. When John brought up the flower arrangement that I had made, I was flattered. Until he went on and on and on, mostly to draw attention to himself. When he suggested that I go get it and show it to the Spenders, I got uncomfortable and resisted. But typically, he would not leave it alone. "It's your work and you should be proud of it. You must go and get it," he insisted. "John, I am not going to traipse through the house to get that arrangement—it belongs where it is. Now please, let's drop it," I said firmly. When he persisted, Natasha snapped: "Oh, for God's sake, leave the poor boy alone!" That cut his water off once and for all. Lady Natasha drifted to the other side of the room, and Sir Stephen and I wandered out through nearby French doors, to take in the moonlight.

The next day Mrs. White returned to New York, but John and I stayed on for a couple of days. Unfortunately, I happened not to be at the house when she left, and later, John told me that she had said good-bye and had enjoyed meeting me. "I thought that was awfully nice of her," he said, obviously very pleased with himself. "Indeed, it was, and I'm sorry I missed her—but what are you getting at?" I asked. "Well, you know, she didn't have to do that," he explained. Huh? "But why wouldn't she do it? She struck me as a thoughtful person with good manners. Did I not deserve a good-bye because I'm a peon?" John said I was being uppity and vanished in a queenly huff. I was not being uppity. I was being the person my parents reared.

I may not be a literary icon with a title, and I'm certainly
no billionaire with a house in Provence, but I'd be willing to
bet that I could show Mrs. White a nice time on my narrow
little porch in the Catskills. When all is said and done, the
good life has far less to do with money than it does with
style, awareness, and gratefulness. I'd be lying through my
teeth if I were to say I hadn't been bowled over by Mrs.
White's glamorous life and the most exquisite country

house I'll probably ever see. But the chances of my having such a life are beyond zilch, and the last thing I'd want to spend my time on earth doing is reaching and grabbing for something that's not right for me, while the sun rises and sets on one fruitless day after another. Black truffle omelets are wonderful—everybody ought to have them at least once—but so is a fried egg on toast with a pile of greens on the side. And if the egg is perfectly cooked and perched on a good piece of bread, and the salad is fresh and alive, then who cares about black truffles. Even then, it's not nearly so good unless you *really* see the plate of food before you and know how lucky you are to not be hungry in the world. If the food happens to be well presented on a lovely plate, and you have a clean, cloth napkin, a lit candle nearby, and a jug of daisies to pretty things up, you're fortunate. And if you have a garden of your very own, from which the greens on your plate came, you're in sweet clover. But if you are also sitting across the table from a dear friend or someone you love who is eating his own fried egg and appears to be happy in your home, well, then, you've simply crossed into paradise.

My friend Sonny used to say that the most civilized thing people had figured out to do together was to gather at the table and eat. And it can be done well without breaking your neck. Oh, I don't mean you can just open a can of Bennie-Wennies and expect people to be satisfied. I only mean that a meal can be very simple, even plain, and still be a success, as long as it's done carefully, consciously, and with love.

I remember the first time my friend Michael came from North Carolina for a weekend visit. He flew to Albany late

one Friday afternoon, rented a car, and drove to my house
that night. All day I couldn't wait to see him. I cut flowers in
the garden as soon as I got up and placed them in the
guestroom and on the porch. But it was a busy workday, so
there was no time to plan an elaborate meal—not that I usually do. I decided on pasta with garlic and herbs, green
salad, white wine, and peach crisp. Then I got on with my
day. That evening, as I readied the porch and prepared dinner, I thought about Michael driving in the dark night
through unfamiliar mountains, and wished for his safety. It
felt so good, like magic, really, to be cooking for my dear
friend while hoping the meal would nourish and satisfy him.
When he arrived I was in heaven and we spent the next
hours catching up and telling stories. I can still see us sitting
on the porch at midnight, listening to the silky voice of
Dusty Springfield drifting from the CD player.

I thought once that I was going to get to cook for
Rosemary Verey, the late English gardener who inspired so
many people with her beautiful garden, her many books,
and the way she lived her life. She had seen my garden in a
magazine that listed my phone number, and she simply
"rang up." I came in one Saturday night to find her voice
message on my machine. "Mr. Riddle, it's Rosemary Verey,"
she had said, just like that. I just about fell to the floor and
played the message over at least ten times. Then I called my
friend Seth up the road and said, 'Listen to this, you are
going to drop your teeth."

She had called to ask if she could get slides of the garden.
She went on to say that she was soon to be traveling in
upstate New York and wondered if she might visit. I called

her back the next day (she had just come in from church) and we chatted for ages. I realized right off the bat that she had a map out, trying to locate Phoenicia. Good heavens, I thought, She's actually coming. When I told her I couldn't wait to meet her (actually, we had met previously, at a lecture she had given, but I didn't bring it up), she said, "Oh, I can't wait to meet you, either. I love you already." "I'll make lunch on the porch," I said. "Oh, you cook?" she asked. "I do, indeed," I answered, "and I'm not half bad at it, either."

Naturally, I ran my mouth to every Tom, Dick, and Harry I'd ever met: "She's coming, she's coming." But she didn't. When I called her back a few weeks later to see what had happened, she was polite but distracted, and said something about "hoping to work it out." Oh, well, at least she had called. That was enough to thrill me for a lifetime.

When she died in her eighties a few weeks ago, it was Seth who alerted me to it. Out in the garden I wondered if recently departed souls could journey where they wish. I've yet to lure my friend Ricks here from Long Island, but when I succeed I'll try and do better than a fried egg on toast. At the very least, I'll be sure his pebbles are washed and ready when he steps onto the porch.

the view

ONE SUMMER AFTERNOON a few years ago, a young couple and their child were in my garden during a tour organized by a local arts group. The little boy, who was named Brent, looked to be about eight years old and was cute as a button. He asked me if he could use my bathroom. I said, "Why, certainly you may, young man." And off he went to do his business. My sister and her husband happened to be visiting from South Carolina and were in the house at the time. Phyllis told me later that when the boy came out of the bathroom, he looked around disapprovingly at the rooms of my tiny cottage, turned up his nose, and asked her, "Who lives *here*?" "My brother, that's who, and that's *his* garden outside," she answered tersely. "Well," he sniffed, "*I* practically live in a *mansion*." "Well, my brother doesn't,"

Phyllis stated. And she sent the rude child from the house at once.

A few weeks later, I was in my friend Cal's apartment in New York, where the TV was tuned to Rosie O'Donnell, and she was having a discussion with a group of children on her show. I kept wondering why one of them—a very precocious boy who was trying to grab all the attention by answering every question—looked so familiar to me, when suddenly, O'Donnell called him by name. It was Brent! I told Cal the story of the spoiled child who had lowered his drawers— and his standards—long enough to pee in my humble toilet, and said I certainly hoped the little creature would someday learn a few manners to go with his love of mansions. And that his mother would someday learn how to behave in a garden. Because while in mine, she had dragged her feet, with about as much grace as a bull in a china shop, through a large clump of pastel corn poppies that were doing nothing but sitting there, looking absolutely fabulous. I was wrecked, and so were my poppies.

Little Brent's offensive behavior can't have been his fault entirely. He'd obviously had too much, too soon, in his young life. The very idea of an eight-year-old boy being put off by a tiny house is one that actually saddens me. Many years ago, shortly after I returned from my student year in England, I rented a wonderful house in the foothills of the Blue Ridge Mountains in South Carolina. It had good hardwood floors and the sweetest tin roof you've ever seen, and it was even smaller than my present cottage. I'll never forget when some of my nephews and nieces visited. They were fascinated by the diminutiveness of the house. "The children had a fit and can't wait to come back," Phyllis had said later. The last time I drove by the clapboard house, less than a year ago, it had not changed a drop—still mushroom-colored with pale blue shutters and still sitting on a green knoll. I wonder if it's been bought and how much the monthly rent has changed from $175.

My little red shack is a far cry from a mansion, there's no getting round that. Oh, yes, there are a few cracks in the walls, and the bathroom commode is beginning to list alarmingly to one side (I hope I'm the one who goes through the floor if somebody has to), but this place is a fine home. And while I realize that most people unused to small quarters would find it limiting, I know for a fact that friends and family who have stayed here have been quite charmed by the whole setup. Even though most of my time, money, and effort have gone into the garden, over the years, I've managed to spruce the place up a bit, mainly by painting and cleaning. I never wanted to *change* the house— I liked its inherent funkiness the moment I saw it. It's extremely goofy in places, which makes me smile. And its quirks and odd sounds are part of what makes it home. When the floor furnace knocks on, it makes a creaky noise that comforts me, particularly the first night in bed after returning from a trip. I think, Ah, home sweet home, when I hear the familiar *ee-ee-ee-ee-eee*.

I'm very excited about my brand-new indoor refrigerator, which I bought at Lowe's just a few months ago. The old one had sat for years on the screened porch, taking up far too much room. Still, it was much better there than in the living room, where it had started out. I mean, after all. It was Ken who had suggested (insisted!) that we put it on the porch. "Child, let's get that thing out of your house," he had said, impatiently, a few months after I moved in. All of a sudden, it was like I had never noticed how dreadful the clunky thing looked. But I had been busy starting the garden and was practically living outside. I never minded it on the porch for eight years, but the new one in the kitchen is a vast improvement. The novelty of it has yet to wear off: when I flip on the night light by the sink before going to bed, I look at the refrigerator and think, You pretty thing, you.

I suppose I'll move on from this place one of these days—but then, who knows? Recently, Ken said, "You'll probably get the whole thing completely fabulous and then go." One day, I was wondering aloud to Seth about where I'd go and what I'd do if I gave the place up. He said, "Get over it, doll, you're gonna die in this house and you know it." I can think of far worse things. There's something special here. Not just the house, but the setting, too. And the spirit of the place— the *genius loci*—which has always informed the garden.

A couple of years ago, a guy I was having a fling with woke up one morning and told me about a dream. "I don't know if it was really a dream, it seemed more real," he said. "There were these little creatures that lived here, all around your house and garden, whose job it was to protect you. Like elves or fairies or something. Anyway, in the dream or whatever, they were all worked up because I was here. It wasn't really like they didn't like me, but more like they were on the lookout for you and kind of suspicious of me. They were very busy, trying to figure out what to do about me. It was really weird, but kind of cool." At first I was charmed by what he told me, but I never could decide whether to believe him or not. Because that morning was the beginning of the end of the fling, and since he was the one to call it quits, before *it* really started, I couldn't help wondering if he had made the dream up in order to set the stage for the breakup. On the other hand, if the dream was real, maybe he had been spooked. I hope not. The last thing I need is a bunch of fairies sabotaging my romantic possibilities. (I mean, really, you guys. If your job is to look after me, get with the program. I'm not getting any younger.)

Spirit forces or not, things are changing in the landscape here. In the ponds by the upper meadow, some beavers have been going to town the past couple of years. The dams they've built have somehow turned the lower meadow, which borders two sides of my yard and used to be merely wet, into a year-round swamp. A few weeks ago, I noticed they'd begun damming the swamp, too. Water is closing in on me. When it first started, I thought, Son, you might have to head for some high ground if this keeps up. But so far, no matter how hard it rains or for how long—and we had some major gully-washers this spring and last—the water never advances beyond a certain point in my yard.

The standing water has caused a lot of trees and shrubs— staghorn sumac, multiflora rose, and wild apple, to name just a few—to die in the meadow. So far, the willows and aspens seem unaffected, but these are moisture-loving species. Way on the far side of the meadow, between my place and my landlord's, is a large stand of tall spruces, beautifully silhouetted against Westkill Mountain. The conifers have been gradually turning brown and dropping their needles; this year, all but four or five appear to be dead as doornails. Last winter, I missed their rich, evergreen presence in the deciduous landscape. This spring, when Westkill dressed in fresh new foliage, I was all prepared to dislike the gray-brown skeletons standing between me and my favorite mountain. But one day, I realized I didn't mind them at all. For one thing, they make me think of the busy beavers, living the life of beavers. And I see the leafless conifers as representatives of death standing majestically in the meadow, tall and proud and unapologetic. And if there's one thing I've learned it's that death is simply part of life, and there is nothing to do but embrace it and find the beauty in it. It's there.

A few years ago, I spotted a young pagoda dogwood (*Cornus alternifolia*) growing near the conifers. This species, which is quite unlike the more common flowering dogwood, has creamy white blossoms called cymes, which are flat-topped clusters like those you see on some viburnums. The plant's graceful branches, which form broad, horizontal tiers, are what give it its common name. I've long admired the species. When the dogwood caught my eye it was in flower for the first time. (I know this is so, because had it blossomed before, it would not have escaped my notice.) I went immediately and got my secateurs, cleared things away from the tree, pruned off the dead wood, and shaped it. The next year it looked sickly from the standing water at its feet. Last year it died. This year I cut the tree down, brought it to the Main Garden, and stuck it in the ground to the left of the gate, where Sonny's *Clematis* 'Comtesse de Bouchard' and a variegated Japanese hop vine (*Humulus japonicus* 'Variegatus') have scrambled into it and brought it back to life. Interestingly, when the plant died, its stems turned orange. Whatever caused this—and I would imagine it had something to do with the quick death of the plant by drowning—the orange color looks oddly beautiful, especially with the mauve clematis blossoms. I always wanted a pagoda tree, and now I have one.

Even though I have what I think of as a healthy attitude about death, I'm obviously glad my friends are no longer dying from AIDS by the boatload. It was getting ridiculous there for a while. More than a few living people I know would likely be gone today were it not for the drugs developed in recent years. The drugs were way too late for people like Sonny and Mark. The older I get the harder it is to believe they died so young. I've wished countless times they were still alive. I'd love for them to see my mountain home. Sonny would get a kick out of the garden. And Mark, a painter who loved bright color, would enjoy all the flowers.

My friend Courtney saw the garden from my bedroom window right before he died in March, with two feet of snow on the ground. Cal and I had gone to St. Louis to see him, where he had grown up, and where he had returned to die. The moment we stepped into an upstairs bedroom and I saw him sitting alone on a lumpy mattress, knitting a sweater for his niece, something told me I wasn't going to be able to simply hang out for a few days, say good-bye forever, jump on a plane, and zip back home to New York. Over dinner one night in a restaurant, I told Cal that I wanted to take Courtney home with me if he wanted to go and could travel. Courtney had come into a dire situation at home. His mother, who was only in her fifties, had had a serious stroke. Her mother, who also lived in the house, had Alzheimer's. Both women were in the hospital at the time of our visit. Courtney's older sister, who lived in the house and had two children, was the caregiver to all three. She was willing for "Buster" to leave. Courtney wanted to go home with me, as it turned out, and was able to travel, but just barely.

Cal had to get back to New York. I spent the next couple of days on the phone with an airline, organizing the trip. Courtney was very thin and frail, and on oxygen, all of which made air travel *just* a tad tricky. Mutual friends came out of the woodwork to help facilitate the trip, mainly by paying for an expensive last-minute airline ticket. The trip was hell. If I'm ever on a plane packed with people waiting for takeoff, and a very ill person wearing an oxygen mask comes staggering into the cabin only to find that his assigned seat is occupied, I hope that I will have the presence of mind to vacate mine and offer it to him until the situation can be rectified. Not one person moved a muscle. Was it because he was black? Were they scared of a sick person? Or did they simply freeze? The way I see it, only the last excuse has a snowball's chance in hell of holding up. Courtney swayed precariously in the aisle for what seemed like ages. I thought he was going to fall. He looked terrified. The flight attendants panicked. So did I. Courtney pulled his mask away, looked straight into my eyes, and said, "If you don't stay calm, I *can't* stay calm. Get it together right now." His mind was still sharp as a tack and he never had been one to beat around the bush.

At LaGuardia Airport, where I had arranged for a car to collect us, Roger was waiting with two tanks of oxygen. I love him dearly and I had never been so happy to see him in my life—there was a halo over his head. Courtney and I got into a black town car. Two hours later, after stopping once to switch tanks, we pulled up to my house, which was knee-deep in snow. From the moment I had begun planning the trip, I had worried about how Courtney would get through the snow and onto the porch. I would wake up in my hotel room in St. Louis thinking about it. Somehow, when the time came, he fairly sprinted. In the living room he collapsed onto the sofa and looked around at my house for the first time. I said, "Wait here." (As *if.*) Then I went to pay the driver. When I got back, Courtney said, "We did the right thing." The words were music to my ears—I had begun to have my doubts. It was Thursday.

For two days Courtney sat on the bed in my bedroom, which has two windows with mountain views, and coughed up a bloody mess into a plastic bag. His lungs were riddled with Kaposi's sarcoma. I would neatly line a small paper bag with a plastic one, just the way he had shown me. We never could get the oxygen right, but he didn't want to go to the hospital. On Saturday night he changed his mind; I called an ambulance to take us to Kingston Hospital. Once he was in his room, Courtney seemed comfortable for the first time. His doctor was remote and distracted. (Where do these guys come from?) The nurses, one and all, were angels—they got the oxygen just right. Ron came from

Nantucket, and Cal from New York. On Monday night, Courtney said, "You queens get out of here—I *know* y'all want to go out to dinner." We did and we did. We left him sitting cross-legged on the bed, playing solitaire and watching the Academy Awards, on the night Tom Hanks won a Best Actor award for his role in *Philadelphia* as a lawyer dying of AIDS. Courtney died the next day around one o'clock. When I called his sister in St. Louis, she started screaming and crying, "Buster, Buster, oh, my baby Buster." A few weeks later I sent an urn of ashes to St. Louis.

My mother knew I was gay. In her way, in some cell, she knew. A yoga teacher said to me years ago, "Mothers know." In the summer of 1985, shortly after Rock Hudson had died of AIDS, when America had kind of, sort of, but not really woken up to the crisis, Mama called me one morning in Nantucket. She was extremely troubled by a dream she had had the night before. "Honey, are you all right, is everything okay with your health?" she had asked, with anxiety in her voice. "I had a dream last night that you were real sick, and we were all so worried about you. Dean, you would tell me if anything was wrong with you, wouldn't you?" It was so unlike my mother to let a dream "get away" with her, as she obviously had, and it took me several minutes to assuage her fears. I wanted to say, "Mama, don't worry. I'm gay and I'm fine." (I didn't actually know for sure that I was "fine," because another three years would pass before I would have my first HIV test.) It would have been a good time—not a perfect one, because there never is—to open the closet door. But I didn't. Chicken.

Eleven years later Mama was diagnosed with pancreatic

cancer and I went home to help my family take care of her for the last seven months of her life. It was a shattering, heart-wrenching experience I can't begin to approach in words at this moment. But how fortunate I was to have a life that allowed me to put everything else aside, go home, and do nothing but love my mother with every ounce of myself. She could not have known, nor could all but a few of my family members—the ones to whom I had come out—that I had been losing friends for years. Nor could she have known (since I never told her) where my okay nursing skills had come from: Sonny, Mark, and Courtney had all died by this time. I would never want to diminish the richness of my experiences with those three men—three of the best friends I ever had—but talk about laying the groundwork for my mother.

She died at home at 5 a.m. on a Sunday in March, as if to say, "I believe I'll just skip church and go right on up to Jesus." The timing seemed just right; she had always been such a Sunday sort of lady. I happened to be the only one with her. When life had gone out of her ravaged body, I went into the next room and woke Daddy. He came and stood by the bed, said nothing for a moment, then looked at me. "She was a good woman. She lived a good life." He knew—he had been married to her for fifty-five years. He went to shave. I lit a candle, called the hospice office, and went to put on some coffee. A few minutes later, with a hot cup, I stepped out into the backyard to greet the dawn. It was a backyard I knew like the back of my hand. But it was a very new day.

My father did not know I was gay. Had he known, or merely suspected, he would have confronted me; I knew my

the kitchen window

father. Two years after Mama died we were sitting reading in his living room, when out of the blue he turned to me, and asked, "Son, do you mind if I ask you something personal?" (What a gentleman.) "Have you ever thought about getting married?" I said, "No, Daddy, I really haven't, and I'm not going to get married. I'm happy." He said, "That's fine, that's fine—nothing in the world wrong with being single. I just happened to think about it and thought I'd ask." "Now you know," I said. He'd sounded like a person who had suddenly remembered a pie in the oven.

I had gone to Mauldin to spend three months with him that winter—packed up my computer and did my writing there. And I'm so glad I went. He died six months later, partly from being worn out and tired, but mostly from a lonely heart. Though surrounded by a large, adoring family, he never got over Mama's death. He was a broken man without his "Lib." A week or so after her funeral, in the cemetery on a perfect spring day, he had stood watching me arrange dogwood blossoms in a bronze vase on her grave. "That looks real pretty, son. Real natural. And you know, this cemetery never looked so pretty till they buried your mama here." I looked around at green grass, blue skies, and a handsome stand of old oaks. "You're right about that, Daddy."

Nine years ago this month, I called my parents to tell them all about summer in my first garden. As usual, Mama answered. After we talked a while, she called Daddy to the phone. "Honey, it's Dean. He wants to tell you about his garden. Says it's the prettiest thing you've ever seen." (I didn't say that. Thought it, probably.) Weeks later, when they came here—the one and only time—my father didn't have much to say about the garden at first. And I didn't think a thing in the world about it—that was just Daddy. But one day he turned to me and said, "Son, you wanna know something?" "What's that, Daddy?" "The more I look at this garden, the more I like it." I said, "Well, I can't ask for better than that. I feel pretty much the same way myself."

And the longer I walk around in my skin, the more I love my life and the people in it. People like my friend Phillip, who's coming to visit in a couple of weeks. I can't wait to see him and I just *know* he's going to like my new refrigerator.

-1972